fashion
sales
promotion

The Bobbs-Merrill Company, Inc.
Fashion Merchandising Series

Color, Line, and Design
Fashion Accessories
Fashion Buying
Fashion Sales Promotion
Fashion Textiles and Laboratory Workbook
    (with Fashion Textile Kit)
Fashion Vocabulary and Dictation
Fashion Writing
Home Furnishings
Principles of Personal Selling
Selected Cases in Fashion Marketing Volume 2
Techniques of Fashion Merchandising

promoting the business of fashion

fashion sales promotion

by Arthur A. Winters
and Stanley Goodman

BOBBS-MERRILL EDUCATIONAL PUBLISHING
Indianapolis

Copyright © 1965 by Arthur A. Winters and Stanley Goodman
Printed in the United States of America
All rights reserved. No part of this book shall be
reproduced or transmitted in any form or by any means,
electronic or mechanical, including photocopying, recording,
or by any information or retrieval system, without written
permission from the Authors.

Fourth Edition
Tenth Printing — 1984
ISBN 0-672-96040-0 (pbk.)

Acknowledgments

The subject matter in this book was organized by the authors. The development of its contents, however, is the result of a long-run exchange of experience and points-of-view with our colleagues in the Advertising and Communications Department of the Fashion Institute of Technology. Their evaluations and suggestions in this writing were a continuing contribution. A special acknowledgment must go to our inspirator and mentor, Professor Jeannette A. Jarnow.

We have used sections of many excellent texts to supplement the topics discussed in Fashion Advertising and Promotion. Two of these textbooks were a special source of guidance and inspiration to us and to many other teachers of advertising and sales promotion. They are: *Retail Advertising and Sales Promotion* by Charles M. Edwards Jr. and Russel A. Brown, and *Advertising Procedure* by Otto Kleppner. Any similarity in certain parts of this book to these outstanding works is purely intentional.

The authors extend special credit to a former student, Patricia Gould, who assisted in the editing and typed the manuscript revisions.

Preface

What makes this business of promoting fashion so different? The main difference between "fashion sales promotion" and "non-fashion sales promotion" is the *product* involved. Fashion is much more than the clothing which you put on your back. It is a reflection of history, culture, and human behavior. It is also big business in our economy. This book is concerned with *selling fashion*. It deals with concepts and terminology which are relevant to the sales promotion of fashion on each of its selling levels. Fashion sales promotion includes: producers selling raw materials to apparel manufacturers, apparel manufacturers selling to retailers, and retailers selling to the consumer.

The purpose of this book is to help make discussions in Fashion Advertising and Promotion meaningful. It has been designed to encourage the reader to raise some questions for discussion.

It is hoped that these pages can provide the student with background information and thus enable an instructor to devote more time to workshop exercises.

We believe that students can *learn by doing*. This book has been written with this objective: to help make a course of study in Fashion Advertising and Promotion, a "do" course . . . designed to aid the student in evaluating whether an advertisement, a special event, or a promotional program has had adequate planning and execution . . . why it is likely to be effective or ineffective, appropriate or ill-chosen.

In recent years there has been considerable propaganda about advertising and sales promotion as being the black plot of the "Madison Avenue Boys". All advertising and promotion are not evil. All advertising men are not dishonest, any more than all doctors, lawyers, teachers, or politicians. In advertising, there is always the market place. This is where the conniver meets his doom. The consumer has a healthy habit of coming back for more only when the promise is delivered and satisfaction is enjoyed. In addition, the power of competition exacts increasing demands for such satisfaction.

It has been wisely said that 'nothing happens until something is sold". The processes and action that promote the sale of fashion merchandise . . . how they work and how to evaluate them . . . are also the subject of this book.

Arthur A. Winters
Stanley Goodman

Contents

PAGE

I. INTRODUCTION

The Excitement of Fashion .. What the Book Is About .... The What, Why and Who of Sales Promotion .. Why Is Sales Promotion Important? .. The Sales Promotion Arsenal .. The Levels of Selling .. Who Is Responsible for Sales Promotion? .. How Much for Sales Promotion? .. Motivating Customers to Buy .. Conclusion.

3

II. ADVERTISING

Media for Different Market Levels .. Relative Importance of Media for Different Levels of the Fashion Industry .. General Operating Procedure .. Types Of Advertising .. Appeals and Approach .. The Elements and Structure of the Printed Advertisement .. Advertising Procedure: Plan to Production .. Cooperative Advertising .. Additional Advertising Activities .. Direct Mail Advertising .. Dealer Aids .. Mat Services .. Conclusion.

30

III. DISPLAY

Importance of Display for Each of The Market Levels .. Window Display .. Two Main Types of Window Display .. How do Retailers Assign Windows? .. How are Window Display Costs Determined? .. How Often Should Windows be Changed? .. Open and Closed Windows .. The Elements of Window Display .. Backgrounds .. Interior Display .. Who Is Responsible for Window and Interior Displays? .. Conclusion.

85

PAGE

IV. PUBLICITY 107

Why is Publicity So Important?.. Responsibility for Fashion Publicity.. How Do You Get Publicity?.. The Nature of News.. The Publicity Outlets.. The Contacts.. The Press Release.. Timing .. The Language of Publicity.. Conclusion.

V. FASHION SHOWS 120

Why Is the Fashion Show Important to the Fashion Industry?.. Types of Fashion Shows.. The Audience and the Sponsor.. How Do You Do a Good Show? Conclusion.

VI. SPECIAL EVENTS 130

Merchandise and Institutional Events.. The Special Events Division.

VII. PERSONAL SELLING 133

What Is Salesmanship?.. Importance of "Salesmanship" for Fashion Merchandise .. What Salespeople Must Know.. Some General "Principles Of Salesmanship".. Specific Selling Techniques.. Conclusion.

I. INTRODUCTION

The Excitement Of It...

A man stands silhouetted against a morning winter sky. His eyes measure the terrain; his fingers reach for ski poles. Knees bent in a characteristic crouch, he is ready for the slope. But this fellow is not a skier. He has never been on skis! He is standing on the lawn in front of his home in a suburb of New York City. He is wearing a rakish "pro"-type ski cap which his children gave him for his birthday.

He is doing what we all do. He is wearing a "fashion" which he thinks will make him appear to others as he appears to himself. In this book, when we speak of "fashion" we mean *apparel and accessories* for men, women and children. This includes hairwear, headwear, outerwear, underwear, sportswear, footwear, cosmetics, and what-to-wear-with-what. All the firms in the fashion industry who produce raw materials (fibers, fabrics, leathers, linings, buttons, trimmings) for clothing, as well as makers of finished apparel and accessories, are involved in promoting the sale of fashion. They are promoting or selling products which satisfy the consumer's emotional as well as practical needs. Do you buy a new fall coat because you need something to keep you warm? Did your old coat wear out and need to be replaced? The business of promoting fashion is very exciting because we are involved in selling what people *want*, just as much as what they need. Our "skier" in suburbia was getting benefits from the "fashionable" ski cap beyond mere covering and warmth. He was getting a satisfaction which might give him a warm *feeling!*

Those who sell fashion must develop a perceptive skill in knowing what consumers will accept—what they need and want. They know that fashion success is determined by the acceptance of those who wear it. Textile designers, apparel designers and stylists apply their multi-talents to creating what Mr. and Mrs. John Q. Public want to see. If the creators of apparel have provided what people want and need, then the promoters can give consumers reasons to buy, based on these wants and needs. Can you think of any manufactured product which is of more *personal importance* to people than clothing? Is there anything we can buy which can come closer to creating an inner-concept of ourselves, which we would like others to see? Promoting fashion is selling clothing to people who want or need it for very human reasons. Motivating customers to buy a fashion product is about the most exciting challenge a salesman can face.

What This Book is About...

The purposes of Sales Promotion in the fashion industry, and procedures used in the various activities, will be the topics of this book.

Change is a most important factor in fashion and involves every level of the business. Fashion sales promotion itself is no exception to this factor of change. Historically the fashion business has been production-oriented. Designing and making the product have been the areas of greatest interest. There remain a few staunch believers in this attitude. The new breed of executives, however, is in the process of developing a more marketing-oriented approach to the fashion business. They feel that equal emphasis must be assigned to merchandising and to distribution, along with attention to research and development, design and production.

Because the large retailer, the department store, is the best example of a firm in the fashion business which utilizes a comprehensive and coordinated Sales Promotion Program,

Introduction

we will use many examples of how such retailers use sales promotion activities to sell merchandise and ideas. The principles involved will be the same for other levels in the industry; e.g., producers of raw materials and manufacturers of apparel and accessories. Where differences occur, these variations will be noted and discussed. Sales Promotion specialists generally agree that the "moment of truth" for evaluating the effectiveness of sales promotion occurs at the retail level or *point of sale*. No firm, *on any level* in the fashion business, can claim success until the ultimate consumer says "yes". For this reason, a great deal of fashion promotion is retail-or consumer-oriented. The processes and action that move fashion merchandise . . . how they work, how to evaluate them—these are the subjects of this book.

The What, Why and Who of Sales Promotion

Fashion Sales Promotion—A Language of Its Own

When a plumber thinks of a tight joint, he does not have in mind a saloon where the drinks are skimpy, any more than a carpenter thinks of a T-square as an old lady who sips tea. And so in the fashion business a knowledge of the specialized language of the field is necessary for those who wish to communicate with their co-workers or their customers.

For example, one important point which might be remembered by a fashion writer is that the language differs radically in relation to the audience. A "line-for-line copy" of a French couturier's design would be completely understandable to the consumer. A "knock-off" of the very same item would be strictly the trade term for this merchandise. Except for New York City, and possibly a few other fashion centers, there would be a limited public outside the industry who would know such trade terms. The language varies because there are

Introduction

so many individuals engaged in various promotion levels of the industry who have developed language which emphasizes the importance of their particular contribution to the whole process.

WHAT IS SALES PROMOTION?

The term "Sales Promotion' has been much abused and misused. There are almost as many definitions for Sales Promotion as there are Sales Promotion practitioners. It all depends upon whom you ask. Retailers, manufacturers and advertising agencies each have their own version. Manufacturers regard sales promotion as a supplement to personal selling; agencies believe that sales promotion includes collateral materials which "merchandise the advertising". They emphasize those aspects which complement their own philosophy of doing business. It is usually the retailer who thinks of Sales Promotion as an all-inclusive effort which coordinates all activities that contribute to the promotion of profitable sales.

We like to think of Sales Promotion in its *broadest* sense to include *any activity, personal or nonpersonal, which is used to influence the sale of merchandise, services or ideas*. These activities are:

1. ***Advertising:*** A nonpersonal method of influencing sales through a paid message by an identified sponsor. Advertising appears in media which can present a message to potential buyers.
2. ***Display:*** A nonpersonal physical presentation of merchandise or ideas. It includes window, exterior, interior, and remote display.
3. ***Publicity:*** An unsigned and non-paid commentary, verbal or written in public media. It is stimulated by a business seeking to present a favorable impression for its institution, products or personnel.
4. ***Special Events:*** Specific devices, features, services, sales inducements, exhibits, demonstrations, and attractions which influence the sale of merchandise or ideas.

5. **Fashion Show:** Presentations of merchandise in living and moving form.
6. **Personal selling:** An oral presentation in conversation with a prospective customer(s) for the purpose of making a sale.[1]

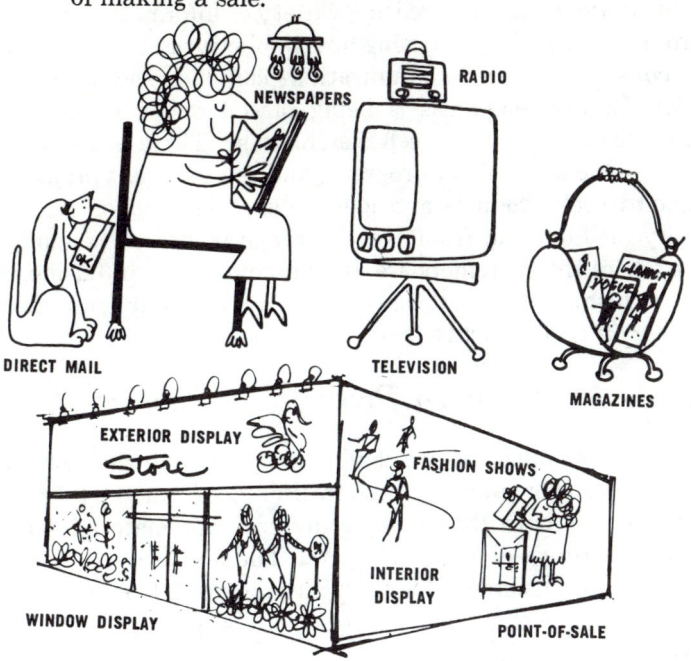

FIG. 1 — SALES PROMOTION ACTIVITIES AND MEDIA WHICH ARE USED TO BRING THE CUSTOMER TO THE POINT OF SALE IN A DEPARTMENT STORE.

Why Is Sales Promotion Important?

All businesses engage in some form of sales promotion activity. The terms used to describe their activities and methods employed by firms executing them may differ, however. With the advent of size and diversification of operations in the fashion business, the coordination of sales promotion activities becomes a vital function. Competition has never been more keen, nor markets more complex. Customers must be sold and continue to be sold if a business wishes to make a profit and to stay in business. It is for these reasons that sales promotion becomes an essential concern of top management.

---

[1]*Marketing* Definitions, (American Marketing Association, Chicago, 1960), p. 18

Introduction

The scope and responsibility of sales promotion in the fashion industry widens and deepens day by day. As business becomes more competitive, and customers become more selective, firms are using an increasing variety of information media to promote through advertising and publicity. Each company must consider itself a communications center—especially the retailer. Greater emphasis is being placed on windows and interior display which can sell merchandise. There is an ever-increasing use of publicity programs and special-event projects designed to sell products and ideas. The necessity for selling in every medium and from every vantage point . . . reaching out to where the customers are, is an accepted fact of business life. The fashion industry, one of the largest in our economy, must sell *on every level* to maintain its position.

Who Is Involved In Promoting Fashion?

For our purposes, we shall classify firms in the fashion industry as either *producers* or *retailers* of clothing. The *producers* include both the manufacturers of raw materials and the manufacturers of finished apparel. The *retailers* sell finished apparel to consumers. They are all promoting fashion.

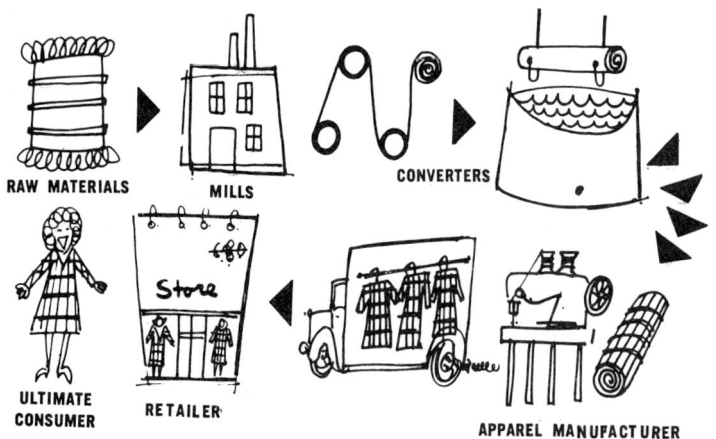

FIG. 2 — THE FLOW OF SALES PROMOTION FROM RAW MATERIALS PRODUCER TO APPAREL MANUFACTURER TO ULTIMATE CONSUMER.

At every stage in the marketing of fashion, *someone is selling*. His customer is the purchaser in the company next in line in the marketing process. Farmers sell their natural fibers (cotton, wool), and chemical plants sell their man-made fibers to textile mills. The mills spin, weave or knit fiber into finished or unfinished fabric. Fab. :s are sold as "gray goods" to converters who bleach, dye and finish them for sale to apparel manufacturers. The clothing manufacturer designs and produces finished apparel which he sells to the retailer. The retailer sells to the ultimate consumer. The whole process of selling on all of these market levels is a creative science to be studied and an art to be practiced. Those who perfect it are professionals. They are skilled practitioners in the science of showing customers how *they* can benefit from buying a specific product or accepting an idea. The professional salesman does not use the "big pitch" or puffed-up words to overwhelm unwilling customers. He is a master salesman rather than a super salesman. He is not, on the other hand, a mere order-taker. The salesman's depth of knowledge of the benefits of his product and the needs and wants of his customer are his equipment for success.

The Sales Promotion Arsenal

GENERAL OBJECTIVES OF SALES PROMOTION

The fashion firm interested in selling its customers has a varied choice of ammunition, each designed to hit the target in a special way, at a different point and with its own distinctive impact. Each activity was developed because it helps to sell certain customers at certain times in a certain way which others cannot do—or do as well. The characteristics of each sales promotion activity were developed as a supplement and a complement to the basic one, personal selling.

The common denominators of all sales promotion activities are their GENERAL OBJECTIVES: (1) selling a product, service or idea at a profit; (2) building customer loyalty; (3) generating interest; (4) disseminating information.

It is a matter of record that many companies which were too interested in general objective (1), and neglected institutional objectives (2), (3) and (4), are no longer around.

SPECIFIC USES OF SALES PROMOTION

General objectives of sales promotion are identical for any of the firms engaged in selling to each other or in promoting to the consumer. All businesses are interested in selling products, services or ideas at a profit. They should also be concerned with keeping their customers sold, stimulating customers' interest in new products and techniques, distributing information of use to customers. Each sales promotion program may reflect a particular strategy designed to meet specific problems affecting the selling of their products. Of the hundreds of different purposes for which sales promotion has been used, there are certain ones which form the basis for advertisements, displays, personal selling and publicity. These are used by all levels in the fashion industry. *Any specific use of sales promotion could satisfy one or more of its general objectives.*

For example: A retailer's advertisement about an improved product in a newspaper may be designed for the specific purpose of increasing the *frequency of replacement*. This will satisfy *general objective* (1): selling a product, service or idea.

A news story about new automated shipping methods can be "planted" by a dress manufacturer in a trade publication such as Women's Wear Daily to make this organization known to buyers. This also satisfies *general objective* (1): in this case we are selling an *idea*.

The most typical specific uses of sales promotion activities are as follows:

1. To introduce new products
2. To indicate depth, range and variety of product assortments.
3. To present special merchandise offers.
4. To bring related products together.
5. To attract new groups of customers.
6. To identify and differentiate brands and/or institutions.
7. To present special prices or conditions of sale.
8. To introduce special themes or events.

9. To make known the organization, departments or personnel behind products.
10. To prevent substitution.
11. To establish fashion authority and leadership
12. To render public or community service.
13. To give useful instruction or demonstration on the optimum use of a product.
14. To reach persons who influence the purchaser.

The exact nature of these specific uses varies from firm to firm and from product to product. The particular selection of specific uses of sales promotion depends upon which general objective of sales promotion seems most important at the time.

The Levels Of Selling

The process of selling in the fashion industry involves many different types of firms selling to each other and *all of them promoting to the ultimate consumer*. We have previously stated that the four general objectives in any case are all the same — with specific uses designed to accomplish those objectives. The *levels of selling* which occur between the different types of firm in the fashion industry, and between each type of firm and the consumer, have characteristic labels. These are: 1) **Trade,** 2) **National,** and 3) **Retail.** The key to understanding these designations, is contained in the following mnemonic which classifies them according to the *market level*.

WHO is selling WHAT to WHOM and for WHICH reason? An example of this would be: a manufacturer of raw materials (WHO), selling a fabric (WHAT), to a sportswear manufacturer (WHOM), for the manufacture of ready-to-wear (WHICH reason). This level of selling is referred to as *trade sales promotion*. If the activity used in this case is advertising, we call this *trade advertising*. The chart (Fig. 3) illustrates the different *levels of selling:*

Introduction

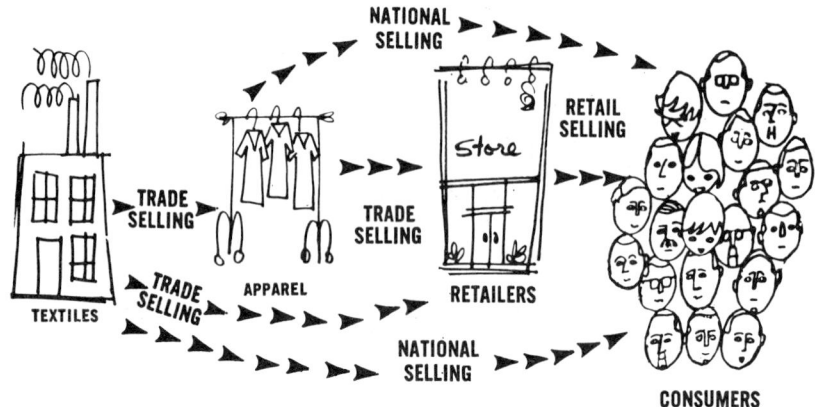

FIG. 3 — THE LEVELS OF SELLING IN THE FASHION INDUSTRY.

When clothing manufacturers promote the sale of their apparel to retailers, this is also called TRADE sales promotion.

The retailer in selling to the ultimate consumer is involved in RETAIL sales promotion — his advertising is called retail advertising — his display, retail display.

Although the retailer has the most direct contact in selling merchandise to the ultimate consumer, producers also promote to consumers. This level of selling is referred to as NATIONAL sales promotion. This is the promotion by manufacturers of brand-identified merchandise, addressed to consumers, who are being urged to buy from retailers who carry these branded products. The chief value of this form of selling is to establish the manufacturer's identity and value of his products in the mind of the consumer. National sales promotion also occurs when a raw materials producer promotes his products to the consumer. The raw materials producer is saying to consumers: BUY BRAND-NAME DRESSES WITH "MY NAME"-FABRIC AT LEADING STORES. The apparel manufacturer is saying: BUY MY "BRAND-NAME" DRESSES AT LEADING STORES. This is sometimes referred to as *"pre-selling"* the consumer.

Fashion Sales Promotion

The term NATIONAL has a special meaning in actual practice. It does not refer to the geographical extent of promotion, or to its quantity. It refers rather to direct promotion from a producer to consumers.

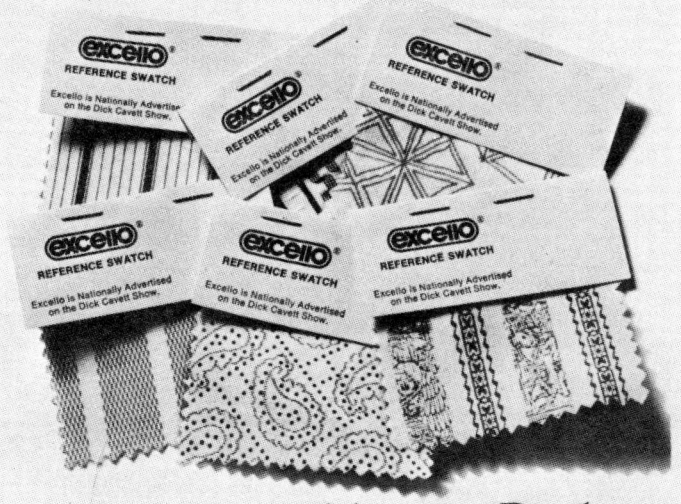

FIG. 4 — CAN YOU IDENTIFY WHICH SELLING LEVEL IS REPRESENTED BY THIS ADVERTISEMENT AND THE OTHERS WHICH FOLLOW?

Introduction

NOTE. in Monocle ad at left, the line, "Available at Bloomingdale's, N.Y. or write" is known as an **advertising credit.**

WHICH OF THESE TWO ADS IS THE NATIONAL AD? HOW CAN YOU TELL?

Fashion Sales Promotion

WHICH LEVEL OF SELLING DOES THIS AD REPRESENT? WHAT ARE ITS IDENTIFYING CHARACTERISTICS?

Who Is Responsible For Sales Promotion?

Retail

The responsibility for selling differs in various types of firms in the fashion industry. In most large department and specialty stores[2], merchandise managers and buyers ("what is bought must be sold") have varying degrees of responsibility for selling as well as buying. They share this responsibility with sales promotion directors, advertising and publicity managers.

Manufacturing

In manufacturing organizations, there are executives and managers whose major responsibility is the supervision of selling and salesmen. Here too, personal selling is supplemented by the other sales promotion activities. Sales promotion directors supervise advertising managers, publicity and display directors whose departments create and execute their parts of the Sales Promotion Program. The concept of professional sales management is essential to both the manufacturing and retailing firm in the fashion business. It could be noted that manufacturer sales executives with their total concentration on the sciences of marketing and sales promotion have developed their skills more thoroughly than retail merchandise managers and buyers who consider selling as only part of their jobs.

The most forward-thinking retailers are now instituting formal marketing research. This is designed to add to their knowledge of customers and consequently, to their effectiveness in promoting the sale of fashion.

Organization Of The Sales Promotion Responsibility

In those companies which have a sales promotion department, the sales promotion manager generally works closely

---

[2]Retail chain organizations have generally separated the buying and selling function and employ professional sales managers to supervise sales people.

with the sales department and/or merchandise divisions. Regardless of whom he reports to, the sales promotion manager must develop a coordinated program. In firms where there is no sales promotion department, the sales promotion function is handled by the sales department. In some companies sales promotion planning and development are handled by advertising agencies. However, no matter how the sales promotion responsibility is set up in a firm, the way it is planned and executed is of greater importance than are the lines of authority.

The important thing is that sales promotion activities be considered an integral part of the planning of coordinated marketing programs. When sales promotion activities are not coordinated, the whole progress of marketing campaigns may be hindered by the lack of follow-through selling activity.

The responsibility of the sales promotion function is to bring about coordination and sales effectiveness. It should, therefore, be reviewed and planned as an essential part of a business' over-all marketing effort — not as an adjunct or supplement.

In the fashion industry, manufacturers and retailers have organized their marketing and sales promotion efforts in whatever manner suits their individual marketing strategy. Sales promotion must: a) be *planned* with specific objectives and policies clearly spelled out ... b) select the products to be promoted, prices, timing and c) *choose, coordinate* and *execute* the particular sales promotion activities best suited to realize specific objectives most consistent with firm policies.

Sales Promotion Planning

There is fairly widespread agreement in all levels of the fashion industry that effective sales promotion comes as a result of careful planning. Some firms have developed this procedure to a greater degree than others, especially the larger manufacturers and department stores. Generally, the larger the business and the more people involved in the execution of sales promotion, the greater the need for a structured plan. The typical *Sales Promotion Plan* contains the following elements:

Introduction

Sales Promotion Plan

1. *Definition of specific sales objectives.* These could include: a specified increase in sales for a period of time; adding new customers to the firm's active list; promote certain brands; introduce new services or present new fashion trends.
2. *The Expense.* It is necessary to determine how much money will be needed to cover the expenses of the plan — so that the cost and the resultant benefits can be evaluated.
3. *The Keynote.* The basic promotional idea for the plan must be created and developed. Often the "idea" is adapted from past successes of the business — or from traditional events which have proved effective. Whatever is decided, the plan should center on a single keynote designed to accomplish the previously stated sales objective. Every activity planned should support this keynote.
4. *The Activities.* Decision must be made as to which selling activity can best do the job. The combination of the various sales promotion activities appropriate to the plan, must be outlined and scheduled. The thoughtful coordination of these activities to complement and supplement each other for maximum selling impact is essential.
5. *Responsibility.* The assignment of responsibility and duty to specific people and departments. Too often a program is outlined and begun with no clear-cut assignment of responsibility. This is a good way *"not to get off the ground."*

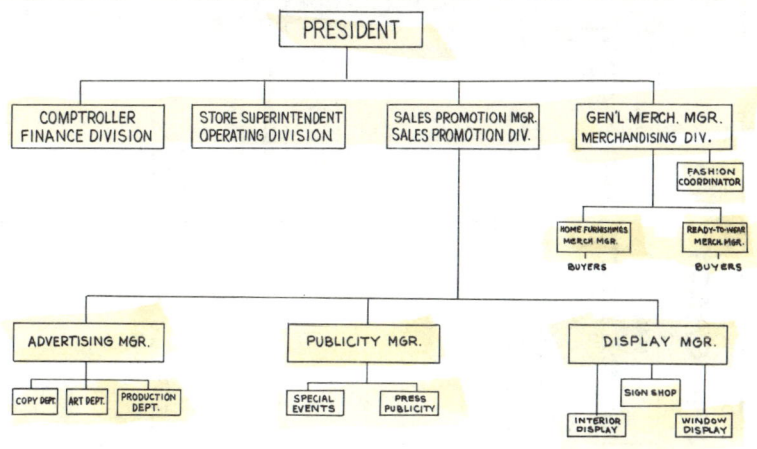

FIG. 5 — ORGANIZATIONAL STRUCTURE OF A RETAIL SALES PROMOTION DIVISION AND ITS RELATIONSHIP TO STORE ORGANIZATION

FIG. 6 — ONE OF THE MOST WIDELY ACCLAIMED RETAIL ADS EVER WRITTEN, BY DOYLE, DANE AND BERNBACH FOR OHRBACH'S.

FIG. 7 — A LONG RANGE SALES PROMOTION PLANNING CHART. (FROM THE N.R.M.A. SALES PROMOTION CALENDAR).

Introduction

Any company's sales promotion planning is of paramount concern to all levels and areas of management. A firm must make and sell its products at a profit to stay in business. Selling the company's product is the responsibility of sales promotion. Developing and producing products which customers want and which can be sold at a competitive price is the responsibility of the management and production divisions of a business. Sales promotion specialists are charged with developing the markets where the product can be sold. They must create and execute sales promotion plans which coordinate those sales promotion activities which can best sell the customer — *and help keep him sold.*

Modern marketing concepts call for close cooperation of all the divisions and activities of a business.

In the fashion industry, the manufacturers of raw materials and garments have to sell markets which are more diversified than the local markets of retailers. The manufacturer will be selling customers from many different areas with different requirements. For these reasons producers retain outside sales promotion consultants and agencies to work with their own executives in the planning, coordination and implementing of selling activities.

Retailers have found it more difficult to work with outside advertising and sales promotion agencies, and generally rely upon comprehensive internal departments.

The Role Of The Sales Promotion Or Advertising Agency

Calling the advertising agency by any other name may not be just as sweet — but it could be more accurate. The ad agency is now involved in so many sales promotion functions that the mere preparation and placement of advertising would severely limit its usefulness to most clients. This is especially true in the fashion industry where the agency helps manufacturers, (raw materials and apparel producers), develop the right product at the right time at the right price — and gets it the right distribution in the right markets. Sales promotion becomes an agency function which helps a manufacturer stimulate his sales force, design sales presentations, train salesmen, plan sales conventions and exhibits, and organize sales drives. The agency can research markets or customer motivations and preferences. Dealer aids, cooperative advertising, tie-in promotions, and point-of-purchase materials are planned and produced. These functions are offered by agencies as a full service or a supplement to the firm's own staff. The agency role today is to assist a client in *selling his product*. In the full sense of the meaning of sales promotion this includes any or all of the sales promotion activities — advertising, display, publicity, personal selling.

Most agencies who work for fashion firms are extremely retail-oriented. They realize the vitality of selling activities which get their inspiration from consumer wants and needs. Those efforts which best supplement personal selling and coordinate sales promotion activities are the basis of agency service. The extent to which the agency gets involved is largely up to the client and his requirements. Many fashion producers (especially the large textile firms and larger apparel manufacturers) have substantial staff of their own which perform the aforementioned functions.

Agencies have generally found that regardless of how limited their original arrangement is: if they can really help a client, they are gradually asked to do more and more. A good agency is considered a staff element in the organizational structure of many firms in the fashion industry.

We haven't mentioned agency service to the retailer — and purposely.

Here the story is quite different. It is difficult for the average agency to provide service for retailers. Agencies which have been most successful serving retail accounts found it necessary to institute specialized "retail" advertising departments which are equipped to handle retail store advertising. These departments are specifically designed to handle daily newspaper advertising with its problems of quick deadlines and last-minute changes.

The advertising agency which equips itself for this service is prepared to plan and produce *all* of a store's advertising. This, however, is not as common as the case of agencies which

Introduction

undertake to prepare *special* advertising material and research, and offer counsel on planning and copy concepts. By limiting their service, they are not involved with the constant pressure caused by the day-in, day-out advertising and sales promotion in which retail stores must engage.

Several large stores which have their own advertising departments use outside agencies to prepare institutional advertising, while they themselves prepare product advertising. Other stores may engage an agency to handle their radio and television advertising while handling their newspaper advertising themselves.

The most successful example of a large store/advertising agency relationship was the inspired collaboration of Ohrbach's in New York City and the agency Doyle, Dane, Bernbach. The institutional advertising produced by this combination not only stimulated the progress of the store, but is universally regarded as a classic in retail institutional advertising; and the series has been widely imitated and developed into an established and recognized style.

Agencies with clients such as fabric mills and garment manufacturers are also engaged in a full range of activities which help originate, develop, package, distribute and promote products. They create publicity programs and engage in various forms of research. The number of agencies seeking business from fashion producers grows daily. The range of services which agencies render to retailers is much more limited. The problems of handling the sales promotion of retailers inhibit the agency's full-scale entry into retail sales promotion.

How Much For Sales Promotion?

The amount of money which a company spends on all its sales promotion activities is called its sales promotion *appropriation*. This figure (average 1% to 4%), is determined by the firm's financial advisors to top management, who base it on how much the business can (and should) spend on selling activities to maintain and/or *increase* its volume of sales. The general practice is to appropriate for sales promotion, *a fixed percentage of anticipated annual sales*. It is commonly believed in the business community that a business which does not "go ahead" each year is falling behind. Thus, the appropriation for sales promotion is not a percentage of what the company's sales were *last* year. They are rather, what volume will result by increasing sales *this year*. The theory is that the added appropriation for selling will be justified by increased sales volume.

The appropriation is then *allocated* to the various sales promotion activities. Management works with sales promotion departments to decide what emphasis to put on advertising as compared to display, publicity or fashion shows. The next step is the development of the advertising plan, display plan, publicity plan each of which is derived from the objectives and keynotes of the sales promotion plan.

Some firms find that their customers can be sold more effectively by using most of their appropriation for various types of advertising. Some rely more on publicity. The nature of sales promotion *allocations* is a reflection of the best way

Introduction

to sell the firm's product to its particular *audience* or group of customers. The allocations must be then distributed to the different "avenues" for sales promotion which can carry sales messages. These avenues (newspapers, magazines, direct mail, radio, T.V.) are called *Media*, (*medium* is the singular of media). The example (Fig. 8.) below illustrates a typical sales promotion appropriation with allocations to the separate activities and media.

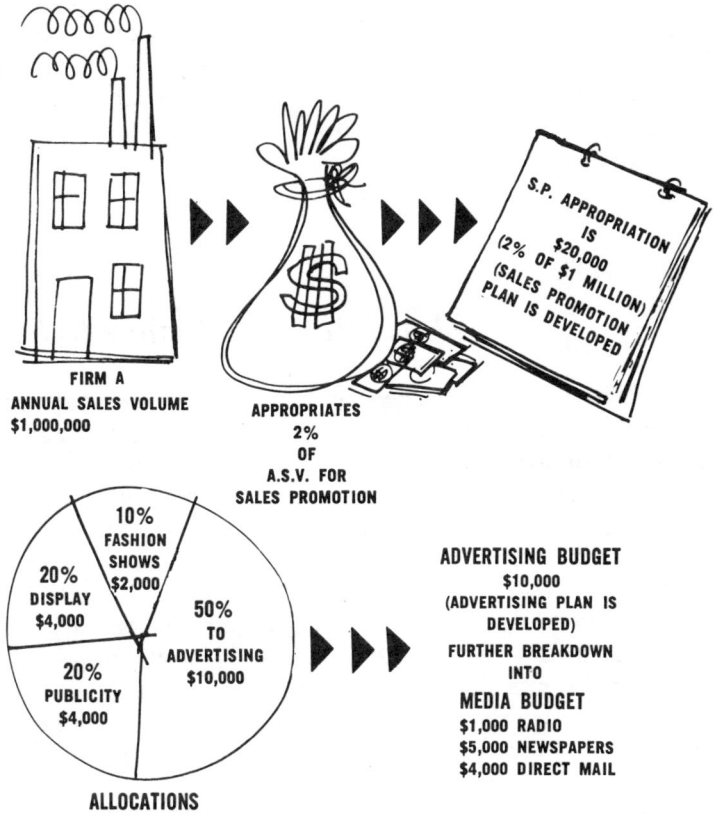

FIG. 8 — A TYPICAL SALES PROMOTION APPROPRIATION WITH ALLOCATIONS TO THE SEPARATE ACTIVITIES AND MEDIA.

Media budgets are determined by an analysis of which media are most productive in reaching the company's audience. These budgets are distributed to product classifications or departments generally on the basis of anticipated sales or profits. A simple example of this might be the allocation of twice as much money from the newspaper advertising budget to the sportswear division in a retail store, than to the sporting goods division. The basis for this distribution might be that the sportswear division *contributes twice as much* to the store's annual sales volume as the sporting goods division. You can see why this should be, if you again consider that the *appropriation* was determined by volume of sales in the first place — *thus, potential volume of sales for a product would be the yardstick for how much you would spend to promote its sale.*

Motivating Customers to Buy

The term *Motivation* has been used in the behavioral sciences to describe a *reason why a person will act or behave* in a certain manner. Certain wants or needs will motivate people to act as they do. Sellers are interested in why customers *act* as they do and primarily why they *buy* as they do. The seller is interested in *what motivates the customer to buy.* In order to present customers with powerful incentives to buy, it is necessary to analyze their *needs* and *wants.* Customer motivations differ at different marketing levels, however.

It is important to consider what needs and wants mean to the seller. Customers respond in their buying behavior to needs, wants, attitudes, habits and customs. For our purposes, we shall refer to any need, want, habit or attitude as a motivation. A need is an absence of something which a customer must have, because he finds it essentially useful or desirable. He *needs* this something he lacks and *wants* something that will fill the void. *The seller cannot create the need,*

Introduction

but he can make a customer more conscious of a need and influence him to want certain products to satisfy this need. No list of customer needs or wants could be presented which is totally accurate or complete. The behavior of individuals varies tremendously. Each customer may have different motives from time to time. (Note that we are using the term "customer" to describe any buyer of fashion. The "consumer" is the ultimate buyer and user. A "customer", for example, could be a store buyer.) The motivations of a purchasing agent for a garment producer are different from those of a purchaser for a raw materials producer—and vastly different from the motivations of the ultimate consumer of the product. The first two are buying for their firms, while the consumer is buying for himself. Would this affect individual motivation? The seller must base his reasons to buy on what he feels will motivate his customers. He will be involved with several important questions relating to their buying behavior. The seller must realize:

1. There are *rational* (e.g., practical considerations such as economy, dependability, service) as well as *emotional* motives (comfort, security, love or prestige) for buying behavior.
2. More than one motive, sometimes many motives, can be involved in each purchase, with perhaps one or several of more importance than others.
3. The seller must also ask the following:
   (a) Why do customers *decide to buy* a product?
   (b) Why does he select one *brand* or type of product over another?
   (c) Why does he select one *dealer* over another?

Motivations to buy can be classified into three groups which correspond to these three questions.

A. *Primary Motives* — involve reasons why a customer decides to buy.

B. *Selective Motives* — influence what type or brand of product he will buy.

C. *Patronage Motives* – determine where or from whom he will buy.

What are the implications for marketers of fashion in this discussion of customer and consumer behavior? For one thing, consumers' attitudes regarding the value of the fashion product are changing rapidly. Today's consumer is very often hunting for fashion with which to impress himself rather than his sweetheart, his boss, or his "world". These attitudes have developed as our values have changed enough to liberate the average man from traditional cultural and social restraints. Today's consumer is more conscious of his own identity and individuality—he enjoys freedom of choice as never before. Recognizing this, he searches for fashions which more nearly fit his own needs and wants, rather than those of his idealized people in advertisements and commercials.

Motivational researchers today have to concentrate as much on the response to the medium and message as to response to the product itself. Many advertisements have contained appeals which were in such poor taste as to cause an audience not only to reject the message, but also to mentally boycott the advertiser's family of products.

The consumer's search for identity is the basic motivational force behind much of fashion sales promotion today. Fashion in no longer limited to the affluent society and the celebrities of New York, Hollywood and Palm Beach. There are ladies in Albuquerque, New Mexico, and Ames, Iowa, who are as much a part of the vast fashion market as any of the "elegants" portrayed in the pages of Vogue and Women's Wear Daily.

The designers as well as the promoters of fashion would do well to think now of the vast fashion market in terms of individuals, not masses. There are many selective markets for the fashion product, each of which includes customers with unique motivational structures and consumer behavior patterns. There are lucrative markets for fashion emerging all over the world which justify their own special sales promotion campaigns from both the producers and the retailers of fashion.

Conclusion

It would be irresponsible and foolhardy for anyone to try to present principles which could be used to solve any problem in fashion selling. Each firm on every level of the fashion industry has individual sales objectives which are relevant to its products, its policies, and its customers. Each producer, from raw materials to finished apparel, must also be a seller who knows the wants and needs of his customers. As a seller, he tries to design a sales promotion program which will present his story most effectively to the buyer of his product.

The planning of a sales promotion program involves the selection and coordination of activities which can do the best job of selling products and ideas. The following sections of this book deal with the purposes of the various selling activities, their individual characteristics, and some general procedures used in their application.

II. ADVERTISING

Advertising has become as much a part of people's lives as their daily newspapers. The student comes to a study of this selling activity with many preconceived notions and pronounced points of view. This recognized familiarity is actually familiarity with the "end product" of advertising, the advertisement. This familiarity does not always include an *understanding* of the role advertising plays in the economic process of this nation. Those who condemn or praise advertising without qualification are in a sense condemning or praising our whole economic system of which advertising is a very obvious part.

There has been a tendency to degrade the business of advertising. A common expression is the reference to those engaged in the business as "the Madison Avenue boys". Justification for such references is that advertising is "sneaky", or that it influences people to buy the things they do not need or want.

While it is true that advertising whets appetites when it is well written; that advertising informs the public of what is available and where it can be found, it is not true that advertising *forces* the sale of unwanted merchandise. Quite the contrary, one cardinal rule advertisers have learned is that it is wasteful to spend advertising dollars on merchandise unwanted in the market place. There is solid evidence that huge advertising expenditures and vigorous promotion do not guarantee success. For example, Ford's short-lived Edsel car of the 1950's; the shift dress silhouette; and the midi length—all heavily promoted—are part of a long list of flops.

Advertising is a social force. Firms that produce and sell goods use advertising to help introduce and to sell those goods. The public enjoys those products, or benefits by them,

Fashion Sales Promotion

or the advertising will fail. Advertising does *not* sell merchandise. It informs and can *influence* selling of goods, services and institutions. This action then provides the economy with not only goods and services, but also with jobs. In the final essence, however, the consumer makes the decision for success or failure.

Advertising grew up with America. In order to succeed in business some years ago, a man thought advertising was the sure road to wealth. Just as America is now involved in the science of the computer, advertising is moving into a highly technological era. Test markets are used for test advertising along with scientific research methods. The advertiser with the big budget spends a considerable percentage of his investment in test programs to determine the strongest and most effective way to spend his advertising dollars. Guesswork can be very costly and ineffective.

Even the man with the small budget does well to engage professional talent in determining what constitutes good advertising and the best medium to use to reach the most productive audience for his product.

In this chapter, it is intended that some of the fundamentals of advertising be clarified, and that mystery be eliminated, not just for those who may be interested in a career in advertising, but for anyone who will have an interest in the subject or will be called upon to make decisions in the fashion business.

Also in this section, we are concerned with the role that fashion advertising plays in the sales promotion of fashion. "Fashion advertising" is no different from "non-fashion advertising". What is different are the buying motivations. Each product, apparel or otherwise, has its own appeals and motivations to buy—yet they have some common denominators. These are the similarities in the needs and wants of people. The advertising of fashion is keyed to the motivations of customers on each of the market levels. In our growing economy, these customers, both trade and consumer, are too numerous, too widely scattered, or too inaccessible to be adequately influenced by *personal selling*. This is why advertising becomes an indispensable part of the sales promotion effort.

Advertising

Advertising Defined: A non-personal method of influencing sales through a paid message by an identified sponsor. Advertising appears in media which can present a message to potential buyers.

This form of selling was developed because sellers needed a way of getting a sales message to customers away from the point-of-sale. This message is intended to bring customers to the point-of-sale, ready to be "sold".

Media and Relative Importance For Different Market Levels

An advertisement relies on some medium or vehicle to transport its selling message to a customer. The advertiser can buy this service from newspapers, magazines, radio and television stations, billboards or the post office. Each will transport an advertiser's signed message to customers for a price. The following are samples of some of the media:

A. NEWSPAPERS, MAGAZINES and BILLBOARDS sell space to advertisers. (Sales messages bought by advertisers in public information media.)

Newspapers   Magazines   Billboards

B. The Post Office will transport your *direct mail advertising* for the price of the postage.

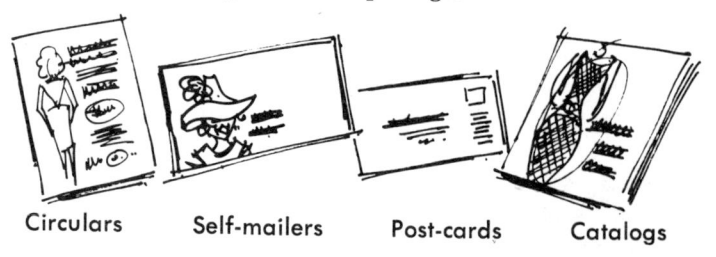

Circulars   Self-mailers   Post-cards   Catalogs

C. RADIO and TELEVISION stations will sell you *time* on their programs for your *commercial message*.

The advertiser must decide which of these media will best suit his purposes. A raw materials manufacturer may find that he can send his sales message most effectively by direct mail. He may also use trade newspapers and/or magazines to reach his audience. Raw materials manufacturers are interested in selling their products to apparel manufacturers. They will select trade media which can reach them. A raw materials producer may also be interested in influencing consumers to buy finished garments which are made from his products. In this case he will select *consumer* media which will reach the ultimate consumer.

The informed advertiser does not select a medium merely because his competitors are using it — or because it is an accepted method for his market level. He does not try to outdo the competition in the medium they use; rather, he investigates all available media to see which best reach his audience and which *he can use most* effectively.

Criteria for the selection of media

1. *The type of customer* sought by the advertiser. Is this message for a prospect, regular customer or inactive customer?
2. *The type of business* the advertiser is conducting. Is the emphasis on quality, price or service?
3. *The characteristics of the product involved.* Does it have general or limited appeal? Is it a new product; an established product with a new feature; highly competitive or exclusive; a classic?
4. *The nature of the message.* Are we interested in selling products, creating advance interest in them, disseminating useful information; selling the institution, personnel or services behind the product?

Advertising

5. *The appropriateness of the medium* for the product and producer. The level of acceptance of the medium and frame of mind of its audience when exposed to it. Would an advertisement for sexy lingerie in the *Reader's Digest* do as well as it would in the magazine section of *The New York Times?*
6. *Location of the business.* Is the location in a high or low traffic area; easily accessible or not?
7. *Location of audience.* Where does advertiser's business come from? The whereabouts of the customer in relation to *circulation of the medium.*
8. *The cost of available media.* The actual and relative cost of advertising in different media must be considered. The media buyer is mainly concerned with the *cost-per-thousand contacts* (readers, listeners, viewers...) The cost-per-thousand contacts is determined by dividing the medium's audience into the cost for space or time. The media buyer must also consider what part of the total audience is really his potential customers, from whom he can expect the maximum *rate of response.* Direct mail is one medium where the advertiser selects the audience. (Usually the more selective a medium is — the higher its cost).

In addition to a preliminary application of the criteria above; the advertiser should determine which media are *most* productive from an analysis of his own past experience, or by questioning customers themselves through interview or questionnaire. There are many methods of more formal research which help the advertiser to determine which media customers rely on, and when and how they use each one.

The media themselves spend much effort and money in *media research* which is available to advertisers. Naturally you would expect each medium to present data which would encourage the advertiser to choose *it.* Nevertheless, a comparative survey of available media research can be useful as a guide to the advertiser. There is also much existing information published by the United States Government, Chambers of Commerce, trade associations and other business agencies which can be studied in the selection of media.

Fashion Sales Promotion

Relative Importance Of Media For Different Levels Of The Fashion Industry.

It is possible to generalize on the relative importance of media for the different types of firms in the fashion business. Of course there are many exceptions because there are so many different types of firms in each level. For example, the broad category of retailers would include: large multi-unit chains; metropolitan area department stores; small city and town department stores; specialty chains; specialty shops. In addition, each of these types of stores might have different objectives: some would emphasize quality, low prices, exclusiveness, discount prices, fashion leadership, or fashion "following".

Despite these variations *most* retailers find local newspapers a productive advertising medium; others use direct mail or a combination of the two. The chart below is an attempt to generalize on their *relative* importance.

	BRAND-NAME[3]	*UN-BRANDED*
Raw Materials Producers	1. Direct Mail 2. Trade Newspapers and Magazines 3. Consumer Magazines and Newspapers 4. TV and Radio	1. Direct Mail 2. Trade Newspapers and Magazines
Apparel Manu-facturers	1. Direct Mail 2. Trade Newspapers and Magazines 3. Consumer Newspapers and Magazines 4. Radio and TV	1. Direct Mail 2. Trade Newspapers and Magazines
	LARGE STORES	*SMALL STORES*
Retailers	1. Consumer Newspapers 2. Direct Mail 3. Radio & TV	1. Consumer Newspapers 2. Direct Mail

---

[3]Larger producers who spend money to advertise their identity for *brand-recognition, acceptance and preference.*

Advertising

The Cost of Advertising Media

Who is interested in advertising media — its costs, its basis for rates? At every level of the fashion industry, every key executive needs some knowledge of the structure of advertising costs for he or she will certainly be involved in decisions and in judgment of media. As an example, a department store buyer will be required to know how and where her advertising budget is to be used. The recommendation of this decision is frequently part of her "request for advertising".

When an executive understands a function of his work, he tends to make sound objective decisions. Therefore it is not the exclusive privilege of an advertising manager to be knowledgeable about media. Newspapers and magazines, outdoor advertising and transit advertising have different bases upon which they establish advertising costs to the advertiser.

NEWSPAPERS — Since newspapers are read in 87 per cent of U. S. households and by 81 per cent of all persons over 18[*], this becomes our most vital channel of communication. There are but very few remote crossroads in this country not served by a local newspaper—morning, evening, Sunday, weekly, or by some combination of these.

The large or *standard* newspaper such as the New York Times or Chicago Tribune, and the *tabloid* such as the New York Daily News, or Women's Wear Daily vary in size. The standard size page usually has 8 columns to the page with a depth of between 280 to 300 lines to the column. Each paper specifies its exact size in its rate schedule which is available to all advertisers. A full page in the standard size paper usually runs to 8 columns x 300 lines per column = 2400 lines to the page. The column in a standard or tabloid page is from 1 3/4 to 2 inches wide.

The tabloid size page is usually 5 or 6 columns wide and the columns run about 200 lines deep. Thus, a full page is 1000 to 1200 lines. A "line" in a newspaper is an *agate line*, usually just called "lines" or "lineage". There are 14 lines to the inch. Therefore an agate line is newspaper space 1/14 of an inch, one column wide. An ad 150 lines deep, 3 columns wide is a 450 line ad, or 150 on 3 (150 lines on 3 columns).

Another factor one should have in mind is the immediate understanding when an advertising manager speaks to

---

[*]Bureau of Advertising

you and says, for example, "you have 1200 lines in next Thursday's New York Times," you would think of this as a half page. Contrary to this, if the Ad Manager speaks of a half page in the same paper, you know that the bill for space will be for 1200 lines. Thus it becomes important to develop a familiarity with language, page sizes and rates. Because rates are constantly changing, it would not be practical to specify them here.

The basic cost in a newspaper rate schedule entitles the advertiser to a *run-of-paper* position, usually referred to as the R.O.P. rate. This puts the advertisement in any place in the paper, chosen by the publisher. When an advertiser specifies the position or page he wants for his ad, he pays a "preferred position," or higher rate. Of course, such preference can be exercised only upon availability. Many long term contracts for such positions give priority to the contracting advertisers and are renewable upon expiration. Choice positions can include specific up-front pages or possibly back page. An advertiser may *request* a "good position, above fold" or "if possible, outside columns" without the extra charge, but this assures the advertiser of no consistency of position.

MAGAZINES — Magazines sell space by the page or fraction of page. A page, ½ page, ¼ page, etc., can be bought by the advertiser. Space in the magazine is often sold by the column or part of the column also. The measurement of advertising space by lines is *not* used in magazines.

Magazines are read leisurely and do not carry the urgency in their advertising expected of and found in newspapers. Because of the better quality of the paper used by magazines as compared to newspaper stock, the printing process can be finer. A considerable amount of magazine advertising is done in color. Color has been found to get more reader attention than does black and white.

In magazines, an advertiser can reach a nationally distributed market or he may choose specific areas through sectional editions offered by many magazines. One magazine appropriately has named this option "magazones". These zones vary in geographical size and each magazine gives the advertiser precise information as to geographical and circulation coverage, by zone. Thus, a comparatively smaller advertiser may find value with sufficient budget, to include magazines in his media plan.

TELEVISION — Television advertising has proved to be most influential of all media in many respects. Its influence is incredible. According to the Television Bureau of Advertising, in 1970 more than 95 per cent of all American households, or over 60 million, have at least one television set. Through network broadcasting, millions of those homes can be reached with measurable impact very quickly. With a one-minute commercial in a single program, on a single network it is possible to reach more than 11 million homes.

The cost of these programs, however, on a network basis is excessive for the budgets and purposes of most fashion-oriented organizations except for the giants of the industry. It is said that the *minimum* cost for a half-hour evening network show for just time and talent runs over $150,000. On top of that cost are writers, production costs, promotion expenses. It is not cheap advertising. It is expensive, but productive for the advertiser whose *product* and objectives are suited to mass audiences.

As an example, a one-minute or 60-second single spot commercial on network television telecast in the course of the professional football Super Bowl costs $200,000!

Television advertising falls into two main categories:

1. *Network or sponsorship advertising*—or in some instances participating sponsorship.
2. *Spot advertising.* This can be national or local. With spot television, the advertiser may use selective markets.

Spots are sold in segments of 10, 20, 30 seconds, or one minute.

All rates for television advertising are based on time of broadcast. The "heart" of viewing attention varies from station to station, but generally *prime time* is from 7 p.m. to 11 p.m. The hour before and after this choice period is referred to as *fringe time*. There are other classifications possible and some stations break the time segments into as many as five.

The technique and details of the creation of good television advertising should never be in the hands of any but top professionals. At these costs, an error in judgment is less than tolerable and every precaution to be efficient and effective should be taken.

RADIO — Radio is an inescapable medium. There are more radios than people in the U. S., according to the Radio Advertising Bureau. Home sets, portables, plug-ins, car radios are among the little boxes that invade the daily lives of our people. Young people are reported to be sharply influenced by the correct choice of station by an advertiser, but radio listeners include every age level.

Local radio advertising, according to the Federal Communications Commission constitutes about 64% of radio time sales while spot sales are about 30%. This leaves but 6% for network radio sales. Time for advertisers is sold on radio in 10, 20, 30 second or one minute spots. Premium time is often called *drive* or *traffic* time, news time or weather reports.

One thing above all is certain. To judge the audience possibilities of any medium, newspapers, magazines, television or radio requires no guess work whatsoever. It can be done objectively by obtaining the facts of the market coverage from media studies and reports made available to the advertiser. Part of any comprehensive advertising budget might should also include *independent* studies which are possible and recommended. These will either confirm or correct information supplied by the medium.

General Operating Procedure

The organization of the advertising effort on different levels of the fashion business vary. The following procedure however is common to any business in the conduct of their advertising effort.

1) The advertising program has to be planned with the policies and objectives of management in mind.
2) What to advertise is determined by those closest to the needs and wants of the company's customers. The selection of products and ideas which will result in the most profitable business for the firm is the responsibility of merchandising and sales executives.
3) The coordination of advertising activities, media selection, scheduling and production are the responsibility of the advertising manager under the supervision of the sales promotion director.

Planning committees for advertising will include representatives from all three areas: management, merchandising and sales promotion. Decisions on policy, objectives, themes, media and budget are a result of the application of their knowledge and experience.

Types Of Advertising

Advertising can best be classified by the sales objectives which it hopes to attain. An advertisement in any medium is designed to sell either a product(s) or the company (institution) behind the product. The two broad classifications of advertising are called PRODUCT and INSTITUTIONAL. PRODUCT advertising is designed to sell products. Its primary objective is the *immediate* sale of merchandise. Product Ads will include *identification, description* and *price* of featured products so that customers can make various decisions before they arrive at the point-of-sale. A product ad can pre-sell merchandise or bring customers to a point-of-sale where personal selling takes over to complete the sale.

Fashion Sales Promotion

INSTITUTIONAL advertising is designed to build a reputation for a firm. Its primary objective is to keep customers sold over a *long period of time*. Institutional ads promote the policies, facilities, merchandise, departments, features, services and/or personnel of a business. The purpose is to seek the steady patronage of customers by convincing them of the firm's prominence and the benefits that it offers.

All levels of the fashion industry use product and institutional advertising. We will examine next, the *newspaper* advertising of a department store to indicate the different types of product and institutional ads used to attain *immediate* and *longer range* sales objectives.

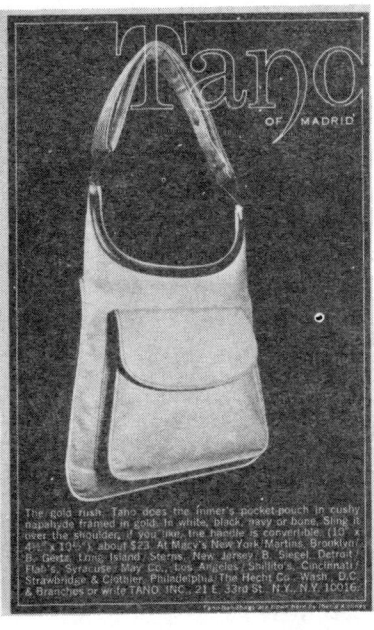

WHICH IS THE PRODUCT AD? WHICH IS THE INSTITUTIONAL AD?

Advertising

Representative Types Of Retail Product Advertising In Newspapers

mays
EVERY DAY A SALE DAY

**Men's Distinctively Tailored
STRIPED DRESS SHIRTS**

Our bolder wide or classic pin stripings will stand out handsomely under your lightweight suits this summer! Impeccably tailored shirts in washable, wrinkle-free polyester/cotton for a balance of style and easy-care performance! Detailed with fashionable long pointed collar, single chest pocket and button cuffs. Variety of rich color combinations. Sizes 14½-17, sleeves, 32-35.

$9

SINGLE ITEM AD

Featuring a single product which is a best-seller or in demand at the time. The product in this case is illustrated, identified (by style designation or label), described and priced.

Fashion Sales Promotion

the paper shop
Henri Bendel

presenting our summer stock/ reams of enchanting papers to write upon/ party with/ pack as weekend presents/ come poke your nose in on 1/ or give us a ring at circle 7-1100/

wickered white paper/ printed in red blue or green/ with matching envelopes, lacquer-lined/ 50 printed sheets and plain envelopes, $16/ 100 name-printed sheets and plain envelopes, $22/ 50 name-printed sheets and address-printed envelopes, $26/ 100 name-printed sheets and address-printed envs., $32/

notecards-cum-pencil/ a parfait of 4" papers/ stacked in a lucite stand. $7.00/

a paper chestfull of party makings/ 100 cocktail napkins/ 50 lunch naps/ 50 placemats/ 50 coasters/ bendel's own bundle/ $9.50/

printed gingham paper/ in pads of 100 sheets/ 4 for $10/ pink gingham with scarlet name/ or blue gingham with navy name/ matching gingham envelopes with scarlet or navy linings/ 100 unprinted envelopes, $6.50/ 100 address-printed envs., $8.50/

henri bendel, 10 west 57th street, new york, n.y. 10019/ add appropriate sales tax for your area—and $1.25 for delivery outside the united parcel zone/

ASSORTMENT AD

Features a range of merchandise from a department or division. Indicates assortment of styles, colors, materials, sizes and prices. Can be designed to impress customers with size and completeness of stock.

THEME AD

Features groups of products from departments, divisions or store-wide which have been related by a *specific theme.* These themes can involve a *special event* (100th Anniversary Sale, Import Festival), *traditional promotion* (January White Sales; August Lay-A-Ways), *seasonal promotion* (back-to-school; Christmas gifts) or *current fashion trends.*

DEPARTMENTALIZED AD

Many different items, related and unrelated, are arranged in separate sections of a large ad to show customers the wide range of goods available. Such ads group many items of the most wanted merchandise into one "Market Place". They offer something to interest and appeal to many readers — a variety of store information based upon their different wants and needs.

Merchandise which warrants the expense of only small space can be incorporated into the departmentalized ad. This offers it a chance at prominence by being part of a large space. A variation of this technique is to group several single item ads together on a page to secure page dominance and to gain attention for each. Another method would be to place single-item ads on successive pages for the repetitive value of numerous impressions.

PAGE DOMINANCE OBTAINED BY GROUPING SEVERAL SINGLE-ITEM ADS ON ONE PAGE.

oduct ads may also be classified by the *conditions of sale*. Any of the previous classifications can also include the following: (1) regular-price (2) special-price (3) clearance (4) mail order.

Advertising

Regular price

This type of product advertising presents wanted merchandise for immediate sale. Its purpose is to keep customers advised that this store has desirable merchandise at the right prices.

◁

Special-price

This type of "sale" ad seeks to produce immediate volume or increased customer traffic through the appeal of price concessions. This could be: a) an off-price promotion offering savings passed on to the customer when the store has made a special purchase. b) the temporary *mark-down* or reduction taken on certain merchandise from a department's stock.

◁

Clearance

These promotions are necessary to dispose of slow-selling merchandise, odd-sizes and broken lots of old stock. Such ads are generally "bargain-hunter" in nature and used only when the particular inventory of merchandise on hand suggests its use.

Mail-Order

This term should not be confused with the term *direct mail*. Direct mail is an advertising medium. *Any kind* of advertising which will allow the customer to place an order by mail *or phone* — (also considered a "mail order") is considered mail-order advertising. This could be direct-mail or radio as well as newspaper advertising.

Representative Types Of Institutional Advertising In Newspapers

Policy — Purpose is to point out to customers what store stands for in terms of customer's needs and preferences. (e.g., — type of merchandise — conditions of sales — pricing — returns and exchanges, responsibility).

Store Services — Conveniences to make shopping pleasant and easier (e.g., delivery, charge accounts, wrapping, air conditioning, cafeteria.)

Prestige — A store will advertise to establish or maintain its reputation as a fashion authority, its alertness in introducing new fashion, and its exclusiveness. Or it may stress its wide and complete assortments of currently popular fashion and staple merchandise. These are long-range efforts to build and to maintain the customer's confidence in the store.

Manufacturers also have both product and institutional objectives for their advertising. They are involved in selling their institutions as well as the products they manufacture. Much of their product advertising involves the promotion of *brand-names*. The purpose of such brand designations is to differentiate their products in the minds of trade customers and of the ultimate consumer. A dress manufacturer for example, might run ads in trade publications to convince store buyers that his particular line of "BRAND-NAME" dresses for fall, constitutes excellent translations of current fashion, offer good quality at a competitive price, and would sell well in their stores. Or he might use direct mail to send a similar message. This producer would also be using institutional ads to enhance his reputation for originality, dependability and service.

His advertising program does not stop here. A *brand-name manufacturer* can also suggest to the ultimate consumer that he recognize, look for and prefer his brand to others[4]. Here, too, product ads in consumer publications such as Vogue, Glamour and Seventeen, will present representative items from his current line of products which consumers can purchase at his dealer stores. Institutional ads to the consumer stress the maker's reputation for original design, quality of workmanship, appropriateness of fabric, color, and sizes.

The producer of raw material for fashion will include product and institutional advertising in his program to sell his firm and its products to garment manufacturers. These trade advertisements will appear in trade publications. He will address the ultimate consumer in consumer media (national magazines, television) attempting to persuade them that garments made from his product are more desirable.

Characteristics of Effective Advertising

How does one judge advertising? An alert executive ponders over this question when he finds that he is responsible to approve or disapprove the advertising for his company. There are many tests of effective advertising. Many of them are stated in this chapter. Most important, however, is the fact that advertising should *not* be judged exclusively on the basis of what suits *your* tastes.

It must be remembered that advertising is rarely directed to the attention of one person who happens to agree with you and with what you like. If this were so, then the fashion industry would have a far less complicated problem in the selection of merchandise. Every dress department might have all simple classic dresses, or possibly all very fussy types; and every men's clothing department could do well with but one general type of clothes for all men. And so it is true of advertising that it must have appeal for groups of readers, listeners, or viewers, many of whom might just happen not to have your special tastes.

---

[4] A manufacturer of "unbranded lines" is not interested in identifying his label to consumers. His merchandise is often sold under the store's label.

Fashion Sales Promotion

An experienced advertising man should have this ability to prepare ads for selective audiences. It is easy to understand, therefore, why an exclusive jewelry shop does not use layout, art and copy similar to that of a credit jewelry chain which emphasizes price in its advertising. This does not mean that one must be schooled formally in advertising to be a competent judge. The point is that one must be objective in judgment of ads. Take into account the medium, the intended audience, the product or service involved, the objectives of the company and of the specific ad. Then, and only then, can one truly and competently judge advertising.

"I like it because I like it" or "I just don't like it" are not logical bases for decisions in advertising.

What makes advertising effective? If it were possible for anyone to answer this in terms of a specific advertisement, this person could make a fortune! This would enable advertisers to eliminate costly research and copy-testing. Our "expert" could look at an ad or campaign of ads and render his decision. Of course this is no more possible than predicting whether a song or play will be a hit before its release. For even though professionals with much experience create what they believe will be effective — in the actual performance or at the point-of-sale, it is the public who decides.

The best we can do in judging the effectiveness of advertising is to recognize which characteristics are common to successful advertisements.

A. *The main idea* is not hidden. The reader, viewer or listener is left with an impression which he can recall. Why was this ad created — what was the advertiser trying to convey? If this is so obscure that it is hard to tell, the ad cannot be effective.

B. *Continuity* — advertising should build upon itself. Each advertisement should benefit from the impact of its predecessor — and do the same for its successor.

Advertising

C. *Identity* — Recognition from consistent style: layout, typography, copy style, decorative elements, art. Some ads can be identified before a single word of copy is read. Can you identify the ad shown in Fig. 9? See if you can isolate the elements which contribute to positive identification.

D. *Relationship between visual and copy.* Any visual (in an ad, the illustration or photograph) must be *doing* what the copy is *saying*. As in a good song, words and music must help each other. The copy *concept* in an advertisement is visualized by art.

E. *Simplicity* — When we add the superfluous we destroy clarity and belief. Shakespeare's "methinks the prisoner doth protest his innocence too much" fits here. The most sophisticated advertising tries to be concise and direct. This does not inhibit individual *style*. It rather encourages an approach to style which relies on "nuts and bolts" instead of "false whiskers"

very Store Name

Pennies from heaven

Shiny, gilty twinkles raining all over a perfectly divine float of silk chiffon. Either in apricot or black with golden paillettes, 10 to 16 sizes, $215. The Evening Collections, Fifth Floor. Sorry, no mail or phone orders.

FIG. 9 — SOME ADS CAN BE IDENTIFIED BEFORE A SINGLE WORD OF COPY IS READ. CAN YOU IDENTIFY THE AD SHOWN HERE? SEE IF YOU CAN ISOLATE THE ELEMENTS WHICH CONTRIBUTE TO POSITIVE IDENTIFICATION.

Motivations, Selling Points, Appeals and Approach

MOTIVATIONS — When we first mentioned the needs and wants of customers we decided to call these *motivations*. Motivations to buy are reasons *why* people buy. *Appeals* are reasons to buy given by the advertiser. An appeal is based upon a known motivation—and appeals are derived from selling points of products or institutions. We could say that the motivations of customers are the salesman's target. He uses an appeal as his weapon which is loaded with selling points (ammunition).

Motivations are the drives within people which stimulate wants and needs. Customers have varying motivations and the wise merchant learns what these drives are, and makes a genuine effort to fulfill these psychological wants. The advertiser must be aware of motivations or he cannot function. Motivations are the property of people. They may include convenience, economy, durability, performance, comfort, responsibility, status, fear, vanity, self-preservation and, in fashion, so often the desire to appeal to the opposite sex.

The advertiser will "size-up" his customer to determine what are his strongest motivations to buy. He will try to convince the customer why he should buy this product, why he should buy this brand of product, and why he should buy from this maker. The advertiser should be quite expert on the subject of motivations and will develop his copy to reach the motivations of his selected audience. In actual performance—or at the point-of-sale—it is the public who decide to buy or not to buy.

An example of this would work as follows:

Pussycat Originals wants to sell coats to junior customers who are motivated by a desire to appear individual. Their collection of styles has been designed with this in mind. Each style has features which are exclusive and very different. These are the selling points which the advertiser can translate into appeals (reasons to buy). Customers who are motivated to buy by the desire to appear different and individual, may respond to this influence.

SELLING POINTS — The characteristics of a product are its selling points. What is good about it? Why would anyone want to buy it? Is size, color, ease of operation, design, quality, label, fit, comfort, versatility, shape, fabric, outstanding? The advertiser must study the product with curiosity and knowledge to assemble all the selling points. Then, knowing that he cannot bore people into buying, he must select the *outstanding* characteristics in their order of importance.

Selling points are the properties of products. The inquiring mind will search for selling points by thorough study of each product to be advertised. The advertiser, or in this case, the copywriter, will use the brains of everyone around to obtain complete and accurate information. He will also read avidly to keep conversant with every market trend and innovation to become expert on selling points. His job is to find points of difference that make his product unique. These qualities should be built into products to afford the consumer greater satisfaction, and to offer the advertiser reasons to promote and to advertise merchandise.

APPEALS — When the advertiser has mastered his knowledge of motivations, and becomes thoroughly informed about selling points, he then tries to match up the two factors. When he brings the selling points to the attention of the customer, and those selling points meet the customer's motivations head on, that is the beginning of good advertising. The appeal is the link between the product's selling points and the customer's motivations. The perfect 'link-up" is not always likely, but the closer the connection, the better the appeal. It might be well to note again the difference between "customer" and "consumer". A customer is anyone who buys. A consumer is the ultimate user of a product or service.

Effective selling selects appeals from the customer's point of view, or what is most important for his satisfaction.

The seller usually concentrates on a single main appeal. We call this the keynote. This should be the unique selling proposition which stresses the most important reason for the customer to prefer this product at this time. Secondary selling points and appeals may certainly be included, but the keynote should be given priority and emphasis in transmission.

Fashion Sales Promotion

It is the primary appeal that can be relied upon to do the big job of interesting and influencing the customer.

The appeal is the bridge between product and buyer and is used to stimulate attention, interest, desire, and hopefully, action.

APPROACH — The experienced advertiser or salesman knows that the way he presents his story is an important factor in possible response. The manner of presentation is called approach. In personal selling, the expert shapes and changes approach to stimulate the customer. In advertising, the chosen approach has to be right for the group of customers to which an advertisement is directed.

The approach is the way in which the appeal is presented, and the selection of approach is the decision of the advertiser.

Because people look upon television as a source of entertainment, advertising in this medium is often presented with an amusing and entertaining approach.

Approaches of all advertising fall into three categories:
1. *Factual* (direct selling information)
2. *Narrative* (story development which includes transition to the product)
3. *Projective* (puts the customer into a situation which features use and benefits of product)

An approach can be developed in one of three ways:
1. *Rational*
2. *Emotional*
3. *Combination of rational and emotional*

Many fashion advertisements fall into the third or combination development. However, it would be an unusual approach which would be precisely half emotional and half rational. Usually there is emphasis on emotional—rational treatment. The exception to the rule will be found in trade advertising in which it is not uncommon for the approach to be entirely rational. When appeals are based on practical motivations such as economy, profit or durability, a completely factual approach is appropriate.

Advertising

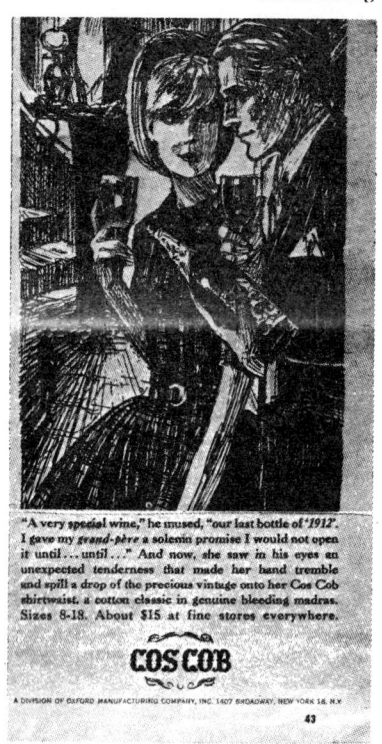

WHICH APPROACH IS FACTUAL? WHICH IS IMAGINATIVE?

Merchandise-Acceptance Curve[5]

Every type of merchandise—every individual product—is likely to move through various stages of public acceptance during its "life". When it is first introduced and its acceptance is generally of a limited nature, it is said to be in a stage of *pioneering*. If and when it wins more universal acceptance, it proceeds to a stage of *acceptance*. Thereafter, unless changes or improvements are made in the product, it is likely to pass to a stage of *decline* and eventually, perhaps, even into a stage of *abandonment*. This movement of a product through the four stages of pioneering, acceptance, decline, and abandonment could be represented graphically by a "merchandise-acceptance curve."

---

[5] Charles M. Edwards, Jr., Russel A. Brown, *Retail Advertising and Sales Promotion*, Prentice-Hall, New Jersey. 1964, p. 166.

Fashion Sales Promotion

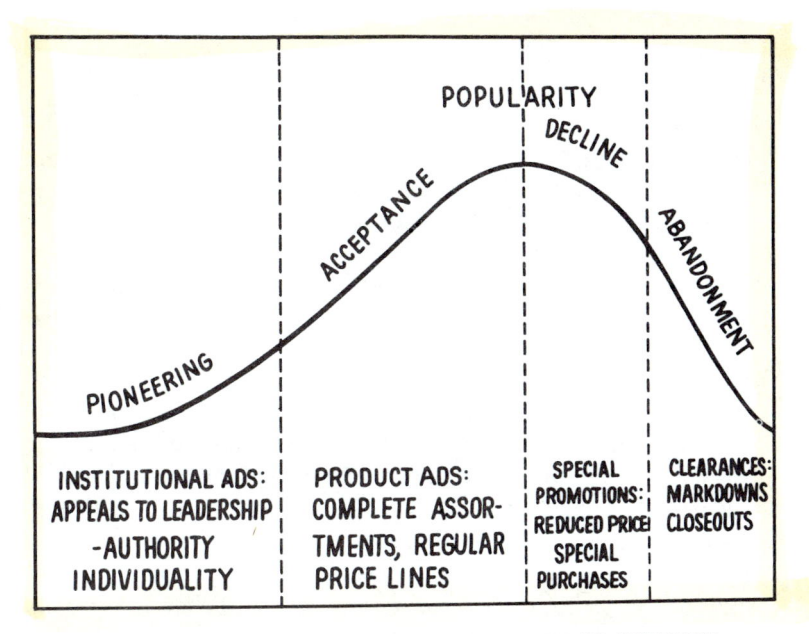

FIG. 10 — MERCHANDISE-ACCEPTANCE CURVE AND APPROPRIATE ADVERTISING USED FOR EACH PHASE.

All products do not trave. the stages at the same speed. Each item may remain for varying lengths of time in any of the four stages, depending upon the nature of the article and the rate at which it gains or loses customer acceptance. Some products, such as novelty apparel may complete their life cycle in a few weeks or, at most, in a few months. Others such as major apparel items that embody design features, may move more slowly through each of the stages over a period of several years. Therefore, the merchandise-acceptance curves of different products are likely to take a slightly different form or shape. All of the curves include four stages, however.

The merchandise-acceptance curve attempts to visualize the position that an item of merchandise holds in public favor at any given time. It is *not* measurement of acceptance, but rather a method of visualizing the comparative levels of acceptance. Accordingly the merchandise-acceptance curve can help determine the type of advertising that the product warrants or requires at that particular time. An awareness of which merchandise is being introduced, is flourishing, is waning, or is dying, suggests whether the store should employ prestige, regular-price-line, special-price, or clearance advertising. (See Fig. 10). It also suggests the selection of appeals and approach. It therefore keeps a store from using a type of advertising — or any advertising — too early or too late.

For example, the visualization of the merchandise-acceptance of a particular product may prevent an advertiser from advertising this item after it has passed out of favor. Such an effort would be futile and wasteful because no amount of advertising can sell merchandise that customers have indicated they do not want. A product that has lost its appeal to customers can be revived only if it is changed or improved so substantially that it wins new acceptance and thereby literally begins a new "life", or new cycle.

The Stage Helps Determine the Copy Keynote

When a product is first introduced, it is presented to customers through advertising that accents the newness of the merchandise and the alertness of the store.

As the item gains increasing acceptance, it is generally offered through regular-price-line advertisements that emphasize the selling points of the merchandise, as well as through prestige advertisements that call attention to the complete assortments carried by the store.

When the merchandise wins such universal approval that is sought by everybody, including peoples in medium- and low-income groups, and is offered on a *price* basis in a multitude of stores, it is announced widely through special-promotion advertising which stresses price concessions on merchandise from stock as well as upon special purchases of manufacturers' surpluses. At this point, the product is likely to decline steadily in favor unless it is modified or improved in such a way that it reverts to the pioneering stage.

Fashion Sales Promotion

Appeal and Approach at Various Market Levels

It is not reasonable to generalize about appeal and approach in terms of *market level*. It *is* reasonable to assume that the "professional buyer" for a producer is more interested in facts than in the projections of the seller. Rational reasons to buy, presented with a factual approach, are necessary when a buyer is contemplating the purchase of $75,000 worth of fabric for garment production. The ultimate consumer *buying for herself* may like to hear what could happen when she wears *this* dress, or uses *this* perfume. "Your boss will love you if you design your new collection with Royal Fabrics" has not been an effective appeal in *trade* advertising and selling.

The Elements and Structure of the Printed Advertisement

What is an ad made of? It has been called "salesmanship in print." The elements of which this salesmanship is composed are as follows:

1. *Copy*
2. *Art* (Photography or illustrations)
3. *White Space.*

COPY

All print advertisements start with a blank white space. The size of this space is determined by the dimensions of the ad. The first element which goes into this white space is copy. *Copy* is the means by which the advertiser's selling objectives are made articulate to the reader. No matter how long or short, we shall refer to copy as all the reading matter in an advertisement. This matter includes *headline, subhead, text* or *body copy* and the advertiser's signature (*logotype*) and *slogans.*

THE COMPONENTS OF COPY.

Regardless of the specific objectives of an ad, its ultimate purpose is to stimulate sales. The copywriter's job is to create the right combination of words which will attract the reader's *Attention;* arouse his *Interest* to read; create *Desire* for products and ideas; stimulate *Action* by the reader. The selling process (AIDA)[6] is evident here as it will be in other sales promotion activities.

Customers are exposed to great variations in copy in newspapers and magazines. Some copy may tempt him to immediate action and other copy may fail — even when he is a good prospect for this product. Why does one piece of copy sell the customer while another does not register at all?

If we could put this answer into a formula there would be no need for investigating customer wants and needs. Copy is a unique skill which is developed by writers who study fundamental facts about their customers, talking points about their product, characteristics of media, and techniques of layout and illustration to make the copy come to life. The copywriter should have a visual concept of his words which will enable him to work with an art director to create the most emphatic visual/verbal message.

The keynote for all copy today is believability. The copywriter must have compelling style to be seen and read—but believability *sells.* Cleverness in fashion advertising is admired by many readers, and generally enjoyed by members of the advertising fraternity.

The hard-headed businessman will often appreciate a clever advertisement, but he measures success by results. Neither the clever quip nor the immediate response is always entirely ideal. Great advertising does not always bring immediate results, and great advertising is not necessarily clever.

Young aspiring copywriters often strive frantically for clever copy. Nothing could be more frustrating to the objectives of the neophyte copywriter than a constant effort to be clever. What is the answer then to the question, *How clever should fashion advertising be?*

---

[6]A-I-D-A is a mnemonic used to describe *effective selling procedure.* The steps are A: attracting attention; I: arousing interest; D: creating desire; stimulating action. In personal selling we can add S: insuring satisfaction.

There is no simple formula to answer this question, but there are tested techniques that have produced favorable results over many years of observation of thousands of ads and hundreds of campaigns. And there are always new and untested techniques to be explored. First, let us establish that if an advertiser says something in his advertising often enough and for long enough, it gets to be known, if not liked. Possibly the most annoying campaign ever to be employed was the whining brat who blanketed radio air waves with a call for "More Park sausages, Mom!" But until he came up with his insistent and monotonous demand for Park, it was by no means a particularly well-known brand. The factory where these sausages are made now has the entire quotation on the sign over the plant instead of just the name of the company. An interesting note on an advertiser's awareness of customer attitudes is the most recent version of the Park sausage commercial . . . Consumers who complained about this fresh kid now hear him call—"More Park sausages, Mom—*please?*"

The little cartoon characters from Wrigley are another example of dominating specific market air waves. The commercial is repeated so often that it is a question of inanity over insanity. It is questionable, however, that there is much of a possibility of Wrigley's suggestion that you can "chew your troubles away!" They even have the effrontery to advise that chewing will make work seem lighter!

And so we have the annoying repetitious copy which admittedly has an excellent factor of remembrance. But this is not what people refer to when they speak of clever copy. A fashion headline that gets attention and stimulates the reader or listener to further interest in the message may not be clever, but it serves the principal objective of a headline. The message in a headline should be "Read me . . . and read what follows me." Such a headline steals attention away from its competition. Now, clever or not, it achieves its objective. The important point to realize is that cleverness is not the ultimate aim of good advertising. Clarity is! Believability is!

If the message of the ad is perfectly clear, and sufficient numbers of people are stimulated to take action, then, clever or not, the ad has served its purpose. Blunt honesty in advertising seems to be the most elusive, most desirable, most surprising, and most effective of all devices and techniques in advertising. When the advertising agency Doyle, Dane, Bernbach was faced with the problem of advertising the Volkswagen, they made it clear in their advertising that this was an "ugly" little car with a great many advantages. The advertiser captured the imagination of the public and made ownership of a Volkswagen a matter of status.

When advertising is completely believable, the message comes through without the doubts that that so much advertising gets and deserves. Fantasy has become so much a part of fashion advertising where the reader or listener is promised happiness, gift-wrapped. There is no need to deny that the public has responded in the past with great gullibility to these advertised promises of hitherto unattainable glories of glamour. Ask any cosmetic manufacturer about the best way to sell . . . let us say, common cold cream. There are creams to make women soft, charming, glowing, elegant, sophisticated, desirable, young (regardless of age), tender, regal . . . and if you chose, a long list may be added to these adjectives which are used in the promotion of the common cold cream. Is this an evil pursuit? According to several writers on the subject of advertising, this appeal to the emotions is not accepted as honorable.

Where does one draw the line between honesty and misrepresentation? Truly, an appeal to emotions is not dishonest. A misrepresentation of facts, exaggerations, promises of fantasy beyond all imagination is pure dishonesty. The public is beginning to be aware of such dishonesty and only deliverable benefits should be advertised. The great problem is that too few copywriters research their product benefits and instead let their imaginations dictate the copy. This is especially regrettable when product advantages are there, but no one has taken the time or effort to search them out and then to write the copy.

Hammacher Schlemmer, a New York shop that specializes in unusual items, has several times advertised a box that does nothing, holds nothing, and is nothing. They sell to people who are seeking gag items to give friends who "have everything". The important point is that the store advertises the item as having absolutely no advantage or use. It is probably the most useless item that has ever been manufactured and sold on exactly those terms. That is honesty in advertising.

There is no crime in adding glamour to merchandise when it is advertised, if there is no misrepresentation. Glamour, color, and imagination are as much a part of life as fact, character, and heart beat.

Cleverness does not cross the lines of honesty. An advertisement can be clever *and* honest. In fact, as pointed out in the Volkswagen campaign, the utter honesty of the copy is the heart of its cleverness. When Volkswagen introduced their station wagon, it was called a "box on wheels". This was an honest description of its appearance. Then, the copy went on to enumerate the many advantages of the "box".

Then what is the answer to cleverness and to attention-getting advertising? How does the advertiser develop clever copy? Basically, the primary route to cleverness is full, thorough, and penetrating research — knowledge of product, of market, of competition, of publics, of public interests and attitudes. These factors are the absolute necessity for consistently clever advertising. Without these elements, the copywriter has no way of knowing what his public will think of as "clever". What a corps of copywriters considers as clever can be a colossal flop to the audience to whom the copy is directed. Advertising is clever only when readers in appreciable numbers consider it so. Clarity and delivery of the message must come first. If cleverness does not fog a message, then there is room to be clever.

The keynote for all copy today is believability. The copywriter must have compelling style to be seen and read — but believability *sells*.

Advertising

What the Copywriter Should Know Before He Writes

1. Complete knowledge of the product or service to be advertised, and the outstanding features from the viewpoint of the customer.
2. The features of and claims made by the competition. This knowledge can suggest the points of difference he should include in his own copy.
3. The keynote or theme of the ad. What is the advertiser's purpose in running this ad — immediate and long range?
4. The copy plan. Good copy has organization, clarity, conciseness and unity. It proceeds in a logical fashion to state its points and then close. The writer's thoughts should be developed without confusion, extraneous matter, catch phrases and ideas not pertinent to the *"big idea."*
5. The editorial style of the publication. The skillful copywriter tries to make his ad an integral part of the medium being used. The publication's editorial content sets the tone for his copy.
6. The response desired. The copywriter must know beforehand what to ask the reader to do. The advertiser wants to sell his product — but shall the copy ask the reader to decide now, consider it at her leisure, or ask to see the product the next time she is at the dealer?

The copywriter who practices his art intelligently realizes that the customer is the most influential element in copy. The feelings and preferences of the users of the product determine selection of the appeals and determine the approach of copy. The copywriter regards his reader as a human being and not as a mechanical responder to a hard-sell pitch.

ART — In advertising, "one picture is *not* worth a thousand words" — but the inclusion of a compelling *visual* (photograph or illustration) in an ad can be a vital factor in determining its effectiveness.

An effective illustration helps to select the audience for an advertisement. It assists the copy to portray how problems are solved and satisfactions realized from the use of a product. It pictures happy solutions, describes features, and establishes identity. Illustrations generate future recognition at the point-of-sale for the benefits which a purchase would bring.

Customers have become more and more picture-conscious. This as a result of the movies, tabloid newspapers, photo magazines, picture books and television. We communicate in mass media through the visual. People want to *see*. Today, the camera goes everywhere to see for us.

The value of the visual in an advertisement however, should not be overrated. Only those ads which are seen and *read* can be effective. It is very unusual for anything but the simplest sales message to be carried by a picture alone. The picture can attract attention, but it is information based on customer motivation which sells. The use of purely attention-getting illustration in an ad is generally too obvious to the reader. The most effective ad uses illustration to fit the sales objective. A picture which can attract the eye, create a mood and then make the message more emphatic, is helping to sell. The experienced art director knows the types of illustration style and subject which will attract certain audiences. It is his job to translate the copy into informative visualization which show how merchandise is used to satisfy the wants of the customer. Illustration can show what products will do for the reader in the *environment* which the customer would like to find himself. A skilled artist or photographer can dramatize merchandise in its most advantageous fashion and in its most attractive setting.

The three major types of art used in fashion advertising are illustrated :

Advertising

LINE ILLUSTRATION

COMPOSED OF BLACK LINES, SOLID MASSES AND "CROSS-HATCH" LINES TO SIMULATE SHADED OR HALF-TONE AREAS

Fashion Sales Promotion

◀ **PHOTOGRAPHY**

BLACK AND WHITE FOR NEWS-PAPERS AND MAGAZINES, OR COLOR FOR MAGAZINES, NEWSPAPER SUPLEMENTS, AND R O P COLOR.

HALF-TONE ILLUSTRATION ▶

WASH DRAWINGS (WATER COLORS OF BLACK AND VARIOUS VALUES OF GREY) FOR NEWSPAPERS; FULL COLOR IN ANY ART MEDIUM FOR MAGAZINES, AND NEWSPAPER SUPPLEMENTS.[7]

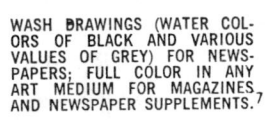

[7]Color advertising is available in many newspapers at extra cost in the regular sections of the paper called ROP (run-of-the-paper.) ROP color is not as realistic and does not approach the quality of magazine and newspaper supplement color.)

Advertising

Illustration vs. Photography

Both photography and illustration have advantages and disadvantages as art in fashion advertisements. Newspapers use methods of printing and paper which are inferior to the reproduction techniques and paper used by magazines.

This is why photography does not reproduce as well in newspapers as it does in magazines. Most retailers will use fashion sketches which are more adapted to the rapid printing techniques and comparatively low quality paper (newsprint).

The photograph can be used in newspapers but it requires special retouching and handling with still no guarantee of good reproduction. Compare the quality of sketches and photographs in your newspaper. See which is clearer and shows more detail.

Photography may not be as "kind" to merchandise as the artist's interpretation. The cost of good, flattering photography plus fees for professional models are prohibitive to most retailers. The photograph is at its best in magazines and newspaper supplements (printed through different techniques and on higher quality paper than the regular run-of-the-paper, ROP.) Photography has a realism and a news interest which makes it highly desirable to magazine advertisers where the budget for each ad is adequate to cover its higher costs. The dramatic true-to-life impact of good photography is a mainstay in national advertising done by fashion manufacturers. Magazine ads use drawings and sketches but to a more limited degree.

photography   illustration

Pictorial and Symbolic Illustration

All illustration is characterized as either *pictorial* or *symbolic*. Pictorial or descriptive illustration portrays merchandise in true-to-life fashion so customers can see how a product looks and may be used. When this is accompanied by clear, persuasive copy, customers can make up their minds to purchase by merely *seeing* and *reading* the advertisement. In advertising which seeks immediate sales, the pictorial illustration is most important.

Symbolic or decorative illustration is fundamentally impressionistic in character. It seeks to create a mood or atmosphere. It may suggest the primary nature of the merchandise but it leaves details to the reader's imagination. Symbolic illustration may also be so abstract as to only hint at some feature of the product or its derivation.

WHITE SPACE

When you decide to run an advertisement, one of the first decisions you must make is: how much? How much you buy from an advertising medium for your ad is the blank space you will have as a physical element. The division of this space will be a determining factor in its being noticed and read. The space in the advertisement which is unoccupied by copy or art gives emphasis and contrast to the design. We refer to this as the *white space* in the advertisement. The dividing of blank space is accomplished by the particular arrangement of copy and art elements within the dimensions of an ad. The working diagram of this arrangement is called *layout*.[8]

Layout: Arrangements of physical elements of copy, **art,** and white space within the boundaries of an **advertisement.**

The function of a layout is to provide a blueprint in which the elements are placed and sized. Layout can help art and copy do their selling job more effectively in the following ways:

---

[8]In the case of direct-mail advertisements, the layout is usually worked on a blank dummy of the circular booklet, pages of catalog, etc.

Advertising

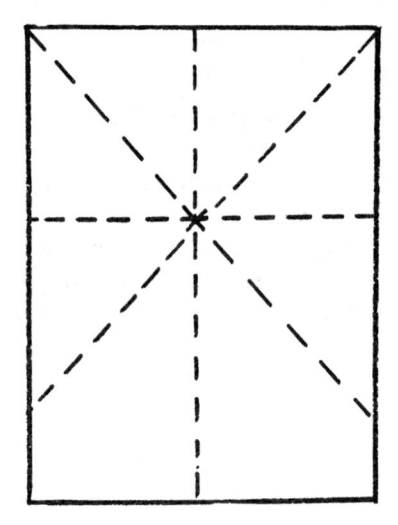

FIG. 13 — INDICATES THE VARIOUS DIVIDING LINES OF AN AD: HORIZONTAL, VERTICAL AND DIAGONALS. WHEN THE COPY AND ART ELEMENTS ARE SYMMETRICALLY ARRANGED IN EQUAL WEIGHT ON BOTH SIDES OF THESE VARIOUS DIVIDING LINES THE AD IS IN FORMAL BALANCE. WHEN THE ARRANGEMENT IS ASYMMETRICAL THE AD IS INFORMALLY BALANCED.

1. *Distinctiveness* — Through techniques which involve unique uses of white space, visuals, perspective, color, proportion and balance, the layout can give advertising an identity which is recognized by the customer. The ad which pleases the reader by virtue of its attractive design is more likely to be read.

2. *Gaze Motion* — The arrangement of elements in an ad can guide the eye by offering a visual path for it to follow. This helps assure that important elements are noticed and read.

3. *Emphasis* — Layout can arrange elements so that some are emphasized over others. By attracting added attention to certain parts of copy, it is possible to present a stronger appeal to the customer.

4. *Balance* — An attribute of good design is balanced structure. Good design has a stability which makes it attractive to look at. The layout artist attempts to balance various sizes and shapes of copy and art to achieve *clarity, harmony* and *unity* in his design. Balance in a layout means that both

Fashion Sales Promotion

halves of an ad have the same characteristics of power (e.g., the power or weight of an element is determined by its size, shape, intensity or color.) From an optical viewpoint an ad is divided at a point about ⅝ five eights of the way up the page. It is this optical center which the eye invariably chooses on a printed page. Fig. 13, indicates the various dividing lines of an ad: horizontal, vertical and diagonals. When the copy and art elements are symmetrically arranged in equal weight on both sides of these various dividing lines the ad is in *formal balance*. When the arrangement is asymmetrical the ad is *informally balanced*.

FIG. 14. — WHICH AD IS FORMALLY BALANCED? WHICH IS INFORMAL?

69

Advertising

Formal balance as the term implies is more static to the eye. Informal balance has more gaze motion, presents a more dynamic effect.

Advertising Production. The process of preparing an advertisement for printing reproduction is called advertising production. It involves the "pasting-up" on art board, elements of art and copy into position designated by the layout. The finished ad is called a "paste-up" or *mechanical*. The production department has the responsibility for effective translation of copy and art into *print*. The copy must be converted into *type* and the art (illustration or photograph) into *photoengravings* or whatever other vehicle is needed for the particular printing process being employed. Advertising production is usually under the direction of the art director who is a skilled judge of design, proportion, color and reproduction. The art director has the responsibility for the advertisement's physical appearance, its design, and its effectiveness in interpreting the sales message in the copy.

Advertising Procedure: Plan to Production

Why is an advertisement born?
What are the various stages in its creation? *Who* decides *what* is to be advertised, *when, where* and *how* much for the advertisment? We will illustrate this entire procedure by tracing the life history of an advertisement from advertising plan to production.

The Advertising Plan. An advertising plan is a schedule for a prescribed period of time, from a year to a week, of the advertising that a firm intends to employ in order to attract business. Its format is usually that of a *planning calendar* with months, weeks and days designed to accomodate the necessary information. The advertising plan is formulated after the sales promotion appropriation and the sales promotion plan (discussed in section I) have been determined. It contains the following information:

1) Dates on which advertisements will run
2) Divisions, departments, merchandise, services or ideas which will be advertised
3) *In the case of retailers:* Estimated sales of merchandise featured in *product* ads
4) Media to be used
5) Amount of space to be used in each medium
6) Cost of space in dollars, (and *in the case of retailers,* as a percentage of sales).

The advertising plan should be flexible enough to permit revision upward or downward if necessary, should sales increase or decrease beyond expectation.

Types of Advertising Plans

We shall consider two types of advertising plan:
1) Whole-Firm Plan and 2) Divisional Plan.

The different types of plans used by firms in the fashion industry are as numerous as the different types of firms which exist. For purposes of clarity we will discuss advertising plans which have common characteristics regardless of the market level. In other words, the following methods of developing advertising plans are *generally* similar for producers as well as retailers.

The Whole-Firm Plan — The planning of advertising is designed to consider objectives of the *whole-firm* as well as the individual departments or product divisions of the firm. When the objectives of the whole-firm are being discussed by top management (committees composed of major administrative, product or merchandise managers, sales and promotion executives,) there is no attempt to include individual product or departmental breakdowns. The *whole-firm* plan is viewed as a basis for the development of detailed *divisional plans* later on. The whole-firm plan, (1) establishes the objectives for the firm for the period being planned, (2) establishes the advertising allocation for the firm for this period, (3) outlines the *major selling events* which may include all or several departments or divisions.

The Divisional Plan — After top management has formulated the whole-firm plan they submit to managers of each division or department, *divisional plans* which are outlines for advertising in various media. (newspapers, direct mail, radio . . .). Each outline will indicate: (1) the *advertising budget* for each class of media that the division is granted to aid in reaching its sales goals for the period; (2) the particular selling events planned by the firm in which this division is expected to participate. As each department or division head (in a retail store the merchandise manager) receives these budgets he uses the information to plan in detail the events which his departments will undertake for the period. These plans detail specifically: 1) the types of merchandise to be featured, 2) types of promotion, 3) price lines and conditions of sale, 4) preferred medium, 5) timing. Thus the individual divisional (or department) plan for advertising grows out of the whole-firm plan.

The sales promotion director and advertising manager receive the individual plans and coordinate these into a master advertising schedule for the entire store.

Let us illustrate by examining the procedure which initiates and produces a typical *retail* newspaper ad:

1. *Buyer's Plan for Advertising*
A store buyer will work with his merchandise manager and the advertising manager to develop several weeks in advance his monthly plan for advertising. We referred to this previously as the divisional or department plan. This plan will include descriptions of ads to be run; items to be featured; prices; estimated dollar sales of the advertised merchandise; the size and cost of the ad, the medium and day of publication. After the merchandise manager has coordinated the individual departmental plans, the divisional plan is submitted to the sales promotion director and advertising manager for approval

and integration into a *store advertising schedule.*
2. *Buyer's Information Sheet.*

The buyer knows he has an ad coming up by referring to the approved advertising schedule usually a week to 10 days before publication. He then fills out a Buyer's Information Sheet ("advertising request form", "advertising copy information," are other terms for the same type of form). It is essential that information for product advertising[9] originate with the buyer. The buyer knows the needs and wants of his customers better than anyone. He buys the merchandise and knows its selling points. He is best equipped to tell customers what satisfactions they will derive from the purchase of these items. He has the major responsibility for selling the merchandise quickly, at a profit. He should be the most concerned with the creation of an effective ad.

The buyer's information sheet in addition to necessary factual information, should contain all of the aforementioned buyer's reasons for buying, and most important, the customer's reasons for wanting the products involved. If a buyer neglects to include sufficient information of this nature, copywriters may not bother to "dig," but will use whatever facts are available. This type of copy is often written by "formula" and lacks the customer's point-of-view. It may not accomplish sales objectives. Figure 16 is a typical Buyer's Information Sheet which is used by buyers in a major department store.

3. *The Comparison Office*

The buyer's information sheet in many stores is made out in triplicate. The buyer keeps the third copy. He sends the original form to his divisional merchandise manager for authorization. The original and second copy are sent to the *comparison shopping department* along with samples of the merchandise. This is part of the system to insure comparative shopping in competitive stores of the to-be-advertised merchandise. The original form is sent to the advertising department after the comparison office has verified that the mer-

---

[9]Product advertising includes regular-price-line ads, special price and clearance ads — as differentiated from *institutional* advertising which is usually not initiated by the buyer.

Advertising

BUYER'S INFORMATION FOR ADVERTISING
(Must be accompanied by merchandise samples)

Important selling features

List in order of importance the selling features (and benefits to the consumer) that you consider the most important reason why the customer should buy this merchandise. Tell us why this merchandise is superior to similar offerings she may have seen.

Be specific. Do not attempt to write the copy, but indicate clearly, and in your own terms, the reasons why YOU bought this particular merchandise. Given this information, we will endeavor to translate it into an enthusiastic and persuasive advertisement aimed at convincing the customer that this is merchandise she needs, wants and should buy.

Please do NOT list price or savings here (use box at right).

1. _____ (Main Feature)
2. _____
3. _____
4. _____
5. _____
6. _____
7. _____
8. _____
9. _____
10. _____

(If necessary, use other side for additional information)

Have you included MATERIAL? FIBER CONTENT? WASHABILITY? SIZES? COLORS? NO-IRON? FINISHES? FAMOUS BRANDS?

_____ (Buyer's Signature) _____ (Date)

Dept. No. _____
Day of week _____
Date _____
Paper _____
Linage _____
☐ This is a repeat ad.
See _____ (paper) _____ (date)
For copy _____ Art _____
General approach

☐ This offering should be keyed for selling starting on
_____ (day of week)

☐ **REQUEST FOR NEW ARTWORK**
List number of illustrations required, indicating item to be featured, if any.
_____
_____
_____

Detailed information regarding artwork must be attached to merchandise samples. (Use Form X2643)

☐ There is a vendor allowance in connection with this advertisement in the amount of $ _____

Fill out, sign and attach BUYER'S REQUEST FOR PAID ADVERTISEMENT form.

PRICE
_____ each, _____ pair, _____ set

☐ I have requested a comparative price and I have sent copy of this form together with samples to the Comparison Office.
regularly _____ usually
formerly _____ originally
manufacturer's list price _____

MAIL AND PHONE SOLICITATION
☐ Mail and phone orders filled within 5 days of receipt of order.
☐ Mail and phone orders filled on _____ ¢ or more.
☐ Mail and phone orders filled while quantities last.
☐ No mail or phone orders.

SHIPPING CHARGES
☐ Beyond motor delivery area add _____ ¢ for handling.
☐ For each additional unit add only _____ ¢ for handling.
☐ Beyond motor delivery area, express charges will be collected on delivery.
☐ Plus small charge for home delivery.

CREDIT
☐ THIS OFFERING WILL BE SOLD ON CREDIT ONLY $ _____ DOWN, MONTHS TO PAY.

BRANCH PARTICIPATION
☐ ALSO AT HEMPSTEAD ☐ ALSO AT BAYTON
☐ ALSO AT GARDEN CITY ☐ BROOKLYN STORE ONLY

FIG. 16. — A TYPICAL BUYER'S INFORMATION SHEET

chandise has been, or will be shopped before publication of the ad.

4. *Putting the Ad "In Work"*

The advertising manager checks the form against the advertising schedule and puts the advertisement into production. He starts by conferring with his copy chief and art director to determine the most effective manner of presenting the sales message. The discussion continues until an exchange of viewpoints and suggestions produces ideas for copy, layout and art. In many stores, the advertising manager will do a *rough preliminary layout* to indicate to his staff his ideas for the ad. This layout can include headline and text copy suggestions from the copy chief. Now the advertising department staff can put the ad "in work."

5. *Copy.*

The copywriter receives the approved information sheet plus the rough layout and copy suggestions. Copy is the "thinking behind the ad" and is largely responsible for the layout design and art which will be used to interpret it. The sales message to the customer comes from sales objectives and appeals supplied to the copywriter by the buyer in the information sheet. The copywriter has the rough layout, copy suggestions, and the buyer's thinking, as ammunition in creating a persuasive advertisement which can be dramatically *visualized*. The copywriter must therefore think in terms of how his copy will *look*, how it can be translated into finished layout and art for maximum effectiveness.

6. *Layout*

The final copy with all its components—headline, subhead, text, description, prices, slogans and other repeated detail — is sent to the buyer for suggestions and approval. After the necessary revisions and approval are obtained, copy and rough layout are given to a layout artist who does a finished or *comprehensive layout*. This layout indicates very clearly what the actual advertisement will look like. In the comprehensive layout, all elements are exactly in place and art work is drawn to carefully simulate the photography and/or illustrations which will be used.

7. Advertising Production

The advertising manager who is responsible for the overall quality of the advertisement checks the comprehensive layout and may (depending upon store policy) show it to the buyer. Once approved, an artist and/or photographer is assigned to execute the illustrations and/or photographs, as indicated by the layout.

At the same time the *advertising production*[10] staff is working with a duplicate of the layout. They will do a typographical layout to indicate the *size* and *style* of type, (following styles pre-established for the store), borders and other elements which will be used in the ad.

8. Printing Production

The finished art is sent to the buyer for approval. If it is approved the art is "sized" or marked for reduction to fit the layout. Additional instructions are sent to photoengravers as to the manner in which the engravings or "cuts" are to be finished. This is delivered with the copy, layout and typographical layout to the *newspaper for* reproduction and first proofs. The newspaper completes the advertising promotion process by preparing the elements of the advertisement for *printing production.* This is done by first making photoengravings of illustrations or photography. Then, typographers set type according to the typographical layout. The engravings and type are then arranged exactly as in the layout. Then the first proofs of the ad are pulled on a proof press.

The newspaper completes the advertising production process by sending these proofs to the store's advertising department. The advertising manager dispatches one copy to the buyer and 2 other copies to his art and production department. Each is responsible for their respective revisions and corrections of reproduction, placement or content. Once these are made, corrected proofs are sent back to the newspaper. A new set of *revised proofs* are pulled and submitted to the store for final approval. The advertisement is now ready for its scheduled publication.

The entire process we have just described could possibly be done in 2 days. But this would be a teeth-chattering emergency schedule, not conducive to effective quality. Most stores operate within a 5 to 8 day *schedule* (working days).

---

[10]The *advertising production procedure* varies tremendously according to medium and method of printing used. The process described here is only representative of *newspaper* advertising production.

Cooperative Advertising

Procedure and practice. A manufacturer of a brand-name line of sportswear may say to the retailer. "If you will run an ad featuring my madras coordinates in your local newspaper, I will pay part of the cost." The share paid by the sportswear manufacturer may be 50 per cent, or any other portion that is agreed upon. This is fundamentally the procedure used in *cooperative advertising*. It would seem that this arrangement should be ideal, and mutually advantageous to both the retailer and the manufacturer. Cooperative advertising has its disadvantages along with its advantages, however. In order to understand these, let us examine a typical case...

A branded-apparel manufacturer makes an agreement with retailers to pay 50 per cent of the advertising space costs of any newspaper ads which the store will run. This agreement can specify the type of art and copy to be used in the ads and, in some cases, the manufacturer supplies newspaper ad mats with art and copy, complete except for the price(s) and the retailer's name. The retailer runs the ad in his local newspaper. The newspaper bills the store for the space and the store pays it. The retailer then sends his own bill to the manufacturer, with a copy of the ad, showing what the manufacturer's share of the total newspaper cost is. The manufacturer then sends the retailer a check to cover that sum. This is a relatively simple and clear procedure. What are its disadvantages?

Disadvantages of cooperative advertising to manufacturers:

1. Stores often do not give manufacturers the benefit of their retail contract rate, and they often charge a rate as high as the national advertising rate. The national rate is generally 2 to 4 times higher than the local rate.
2. Stores often run manufacturers' advertisements as part of departmentalized advertisements, and divide the total cost of space, including headings, copy, and logotype, among various manufacturers. They also may charge for art work and production when they create their own ads; rather than use the manufacturer's ad mat.

3. There is invariably a great amount of record keeping and accounting correspondence.
4. Despite warnings, stores are very slow in sending in bills and friction is the result.
5. Stores that have contracts with papers to use a certain amount of space a month, or a year, may use manufacturers' advertising on poor selling days, reserving good selling days for their own store promotions.
6. It is often difficult to control how a store will advertise the manufacturer's product. Many stores will not use a newspaper ad mat as supplied but will revise material that they feel emphasizes the manufacturer rather than the retailer. In making revisions, the store may eliminate elements which identify the manufacturer and complement his *national* advertising.
7. Much cooperative advertising is not coordinated with the stores' planned promotions. There is a difference in style and content and little or no supplementation of window and interior display.
8. The competition between manufacturers may cause them to spend more money in cooperative advertising than is warranted.
9. Some retailers consider advertising allowances as discounts. Some will ask for a blanket "3 per cent or 5 per cent advertising allowance" for unspecified promotional efforts. The manufacturer can guard against this by paying only upon receipt of tear sheets of ads.

Disadvantages of cooperative advertising to retailers:

1. The lure to buy merchandise because of the influence of financial participation by the manufacturer in promotion.
2. Frequently the retailer is burdened with the launching of the promotion of comparatively little-known names.
3. At the insistence of the manufacturer, cooperative advertising frequently lacks good identity with the retailer's format. This practice disrupts the continuity of the retailer's advertising.
4. There is a possibility that the merchandise being cooperatively advertised is not in keeping with the store's objectives, and personality.
5. If the store buyer handles the cooperative advertising agreement, there is danger that the advertising director may not be consulted until it is too late to incorporate his thinking.

Advantages of cooperative advertising:

1. It gives the manufacturer and the retailer additional exposure for their advertising dollar by sharing the advertising cost.
2. It can give a line the sponsorship of prominent retailers.
3. It may indicate to a manufacturer the degree of appeal of certain products in his line.
4. Retail advertising usually gets a better position in a newspaper than national advertising and is much lower in cost, because of the difference in rates between retail and national newspaper advertising space. This difference in rates is being eliminated by many newspapers and by some local radio stations.
5. It can give a retailer identification with well known and accepted national brand names.

Other implications

A section of the Robinson-Patman Act requires that advertising allowances be made available to all stores on a proportionate basis when the stores are located in the same marketing area. A store is considered to be in the same marketing area when it competes for the same consumers' business. If there is doubt as to what constitutes a "marketing area", the U. S. Department of Labor's Bureau of Labor Statistics will provide answers to any questions regarding marketing areas. Still, there is always the danger of some store feeling that it has been discriminated against, even if not legally so. Cooperative advertising can create ill feeling by the retailer who feels he is not getting his fair share.

The pressure on buyers from manufacturers offering to pay for cooperative advertising can get to be too high. The buyer should attempt to make the "best deal" only with those manufacturers whose merchandise is most wanted by his customers. If a buyer permits this allowance to sway his judgment and tries to promote anything but the most desirable — he could be in trouble.

Conclusion

Cooperative advertising can be of real value both to store and to manufacturer. The terms should be clearly agreed upon in advance, including the schedule of space, dates, newspapers, and the basis of charging. Total expenditures should be limited in some way, as in terms of a percentage of purchases. There should be agreement whether the advertisement is to be run by itself or a part of a departmentalized store advertisement, and whether supplementary sales promotion is to be offered at the same time without further cost.

Written cooperative advertising agreements avoid many arguments as to what was actually in the arrangement. Most large companies have standard printed agreements ready for the dealer. They specify every possible detail right down to the correct size logo which the manufacturer requires for the advertising to be eligible for cooperative money. The written agreement serves also to prevent legal involvement with reference to preferential treatment of one dealer where others are to be granted the same or similar treatment.

Cooperative advertising can be an important part of the advertising plan. It should not be the reason for a buyer to stock an item, unless this merchandise is important to his customers.

Additional Advertising Activities

Direct Mail Advertising

Direct-mail advertising is that form of advertising that is sent through the mail. It is a most important member of the advertising family. If a leaflet is placed on a store counter, that is *direct advertising*. But if the leaflet is sent by mail that is *direct-mail* advertising. Physically the two items may be the same. The difference is in the way they are distributed.

Generally, the first form of advertising most firms use when they start into business are letters, flyers and other forms of direct-mail advertising. No matter how large they become or how many other types of advertising they use, direct mail is usually one of them.

Direct mail should not be confused with mail order. Direct mail is an advertising medium. Mail-order is a method of distribution in which a sale is initiated and completed through advertisements and return mail (or phone call). Mail-order is not an advertising medium, but it employs such advertising media as direct-mail, newspapers, magazines and radio in its selling effort.

Who uses direct-mail advertising? Direct mail advertising is so versatile that it is used at all levels of the fashion industry to sell to prospective customers, active customers and inactive customers. It is used to bring in the business all by itself (this is called mail-order advertising) or to supplement the personal selling activity, or to bring customers to the point-of-sale.

Direct mail advertising is used by producers and retailers for the following:
A. to get mail orders
B. to solicit inquiries from interested prospects, to be followed up by mail for their orders.
C. to help get "leads" for salespeople.
D. to follow up salesmen's calls.
E. to stimulate people to visit the point-of-sale or to see a specially planned demonstration.
F. to keep in touch with active and inactive customers.
G. to tell customers of forthcoming sales promotion events.

The Mailing List. The audience for direct-mail advertising is based on a list of prospects to whom the advertisements are to be mailed. This list is generally not a prepared selection of names which can be purchased ready-made from mailing-list firms. Mailing-list firms are actually selling a service. This service is their ability to gather and classify names of various categories of customers. It is the responsibility of the *advertiser* however, to determine just who his audience is, and what part of this market he wishes on his list. After this has been determined, it is usually possible to develop this list himself much more effectively than anyone else could or would.

It should be apparent that the effectiveness of any direct mail advertising is pre-determined by the degree to which the people on the list are good prospects for the products advertised. What would it avail an advertiser to send booklets on expensive back-to-college clothes to customers who could not afford them or to tell a small retailer the advantages of a quantity buying, or to describe the "satisfaction of making your own clothes" to the woman who likes to buy her gowns in the most expensive metropolitan shops? The first demand of any direct-mail list is that it include only those who are in a position to use the product advertised.

How is the list developed? The direct opportunities for obtaining names of prospects are often so obvious that they are overlooked. Present and past customers usually form the best list for a direct-mail advertising program. Frequently a name will be on the customers' list when that person buys only occasionally, or buys little instead of much. Many businesses have developed effective mailing lists which have been used to convert inactive customers to active buyers.

Another excellent source of names is from the reports of salesmen. Many firms supply special forms for the salesman to fill out. These forms provide information on active and prospective customers which help to classify them into categories based upon their special interests and requirements.

The mailing list can often be developed through magazine, newspaper or radio advertising that asks customers who are interested to write for further information and details.

Advertising

The resourceful advertiser has other sources of current, established material: Directories, newspaper and trade journal listings and announcements, trade association reference material, and government statistical information are just a few.

Dealer Aids

Dealer aids are any of a group of sales promotion material for advertising, display, publicity, fashion shows... which a producer will supply to a retailer to help him sell his customers. Some examples of advertising dealer aids are:

Direct Mail tie-ins. Statement enclosures, leaflets, catalogs, or similar material that a manufacturer prints in quantity and supplies to another producer or a retailer for mailing to his list. On this material a place is usually provided for imprinting the name and address of the dealer, so that the message seems to come from him.

Radio and television tie-ins. When a producer has an advertising campaign either by radio or television, this provides an excellent opportunity to tie-in with local retailers (dealers). If the manufacturer's line is carried by one or a few exclusive retailers in a territory, they may join in the program on a local participation basis, getting their special commercial in at the beginning or end of the show or wherever it will fit in.

Outdoor and car-card tie-ins. When a campaign of outdoor or car-card advertising in a town is planned, the local retailer is told that if he will feature a branded line, his name will be printed on the outdoor advertisement or car card to inform customers where the merchandise can be obtained.

Newspaper ad mats

The *newspaper ad mat* is a device which enables a producer to provide a retailer with a finished newspaper advertisement featuring products which the retailer is buying for promotion. The ad mat is a treated composition material, similar to cardboard or plastic. It is actually an impression of the illustration and typography in an ad which has been photographically converted into "raised metal." This "raised metal" is the *engraving* and the *metal type* which was mentioned previously in our discussion of advertising production. The ad mat is a re-reproduction of the engraving and the type which can be produced in quantity at low cost, by rapid pressings of the ad material under great pressure. This works much the same as a wax impression of a key. The mat is light weight and inexpensive. A 4″ x 10″ ad mat can be produced in quantity for about 15¢ to 50¢ each, depending upon quality. It can be mailed to retailers who plan to advertise either on their own or on a cooperative advertising arrangement. The producer generally sends mats to retailers without charge. His cost per mat is often low enough so that he may include ad mats in every merchandise shipment, whether it has been requested by the retailer or not.

The retailer's local newspaper can duplicate the original engraving and type by casting a metal alloy into the mat. The mat material is capable of withstanding the high heat involved in this casting. This cast is called a *stereotype*. It can be cut apart in order to rearrange or eliminate elements of illustration and copy as directed by the advertiser.

The use of the newspaper ad mat is limited because it is prepared for many stores. It cannot be individual in its treatment of art, layout and copy. It is therefore rarely used by stores which have their own definitive style. The small retailer, who is not equipped or cannot afford to plan and produce effective newspaper ads, considers the ad mat an important dealer aid. Even in his case, he will often use parts of the ad mat, and by revising and substituting elements will make the finished advertisement more individual. The various stages involved in producing mats from original engravings and type, the casting of the stereotype from the mat, and the processing of the stereotype into the newspaper printing system result in a loss of fidelity in reproduction. This is another reason why newspaper ad mats have limited use. For hundreds of small retailers however, the ad mat is an answer to getting better art and copy at a lower cost than they could possibly obtain themselves.

Conclusion

This is by no means a complete picture of advertising in the fashion industry. It is an overview which includes concepts, procedures and terminology organized to provide the student with a background for further analysis and discussion.

III – DISPLAY

Display defined: A nonpersonal physical presentation of merchandise or ideas. It includes window, exterior, interior, and remote display.

Importance of Display For Each of the Market Levels

Producers and retailers both use display as a selling activity. Producers, however, are not so much concerned with display at their own point-of-sale as are retailers. Most of them do not have windows or anything else which might parallel the window display of a retailer. Many manufacturers will present displays of products, services and ideas in their showrooms — a form of interior display. In many cases these are retail-oriented to give window and interior display suggestions to their retail dealers. Producers have also developed a large range of exterior, window and interior (point-of-sale) displays which they supply to retailers in order to help them sell their products. Some of these include: Outdoor overhead signs, door signs, window props and material, window banners and decals, interior overhead signs and banners, wall displays, shelf strips, counter cards, counter and wall racks and cases, floor racks, floor stands, and floor cases. We mention all of these because of the growing prominence of this important form of manufacturer-to-retailer aid which sales promotion people call *"dealer aids."*

In our discussion of display in this section we will concentrate on the major uses of *window and interior display* by the retailer.

Window and Interior Display

No matter what kinds of merchandise a store handles or to what classes of people it caters, no matter what its type, size or financial strength, window display is among the store's most valuable media for delivering a selling message to potential customers. Many stores consider window display the most important of all forms of sales promotion. Often in fact, window display is the only form of promotion used, other than interior display. The high rentals paid by large department stores for sites affording good window display possibilities indicate the value that retailers attach to window display.

Window and interior displays are forms of sales promotion that are almost indispensable to every store. Window display helps a retailer to make sales inside the store by showing potential customers, through attractive window displays, the kinds of wanted merchandise carried in stock. Window displays, moreover, are at work while the store is closed, but interior displays work only while the store is open.[11] Both window and interior displays have advantages over other sales promotion activities in that they show the merchandise itself, rather than pictures or written descriptions of the goods. Numerous attention-getting devices such as color and mechanical motion can be utilized to present the merchandise most attractively. While other media reach prospective purchasers away from the point-of-sale, displays exhibit merchandise in the store itself. As a result, intentions to buy can be easily converted into actual purchases.

Window and interior displays have one very definite limitation which should not be overlooked. Because of their fixed position, displays are not seen unless people visit the store intentionally, pass the displays accidentally, or are attracted to the store by advertising or sales promotion designed to bring them there. Progressive retailers who wish to extend their trading areas and to increase their sales volume therefore recognize the necessity for supplementing displays with

---

[11] An exception is in the case of the "open window" display which will be discussed later in this section.

other forms of sales promotion (advertising, publicity, special events) which reach out for customers beyond the sidewalks surrounding their stores.

Exterior Display

Sometimes called *facade* display, this is largely for atmospheric and decorative purposes. Exterior display is most often ornamental and sometimes informational. It consists of material which is displayed on the *outside* of a store or business building.

Some examples are: Christmas trees; colored awnings; potted plants, or decorative messages ("anniversary sales"). Examples of some uses of exterior display would be to "dress-up" a store for a special event, a seasonal promotion or a store-wide theme.

Remote Display

This is the only type of display which is "remote" or *away from the point-of-sale*. It is a display which a manufacturer or a retailer will set up in a hotel lobby, exhibit hall or airline terminal. It has the advantage of moving away from the point-of-sale to reach customers; the disadvantage of not being able to convert intentions to buy into immediate purchases.

Window Display

Importance of Window Display

Windows are the "looks" and personality of a store. They provide the important first impression that a store can make on the customer. Windows function as an introduction of the seller to the purchaser. When they are used effectively they can contribute considerably to a store's traffic and sales volume. There have been many surveys to prove the effectiveness of window display. These have shown that the percentage of customers stopped by windows, out of all who are passing-by, compares favorably to the percentage of customers from the total circulation of an advertisement, who read and respond to the ad.

If you compare window display and advertising further, you can see several other common denominators. They have the same fundamental purposes. either (1) to sell merchandise immediately or (2) to build a reputation over a longer period. In other words, as in advertising, there are "product and institutional" type windows. They must both fight for attention and interest yet register their impressions rapidly and emphatically. In the case of printed advertising we are dealing with two dimensions. In the case of window display we are operating in three dimensions. We could say, therefore, that some of the principles which make an advertisement effective also make a window display effective.

Advantages of window display over advertising. Window display does have some obvious advantages over advertising[12] as a sales promotion activity. (1) It is used at the point-of-sale. (2) Display presents the merchandise itself, life-size, in natural color, with fabric texture and other detail easier for the customer to see. (3) Window shopping is a form of "entertainment" — it is a veritable "wishing world" for the customer who finds it easy to identify with the attractive mannikins. Good display is capable of creating strong desire for merchandise even in the "just looking" customer.

Should Window Display Duplicate Advertising?

Some stores regard window display as an activity separate from other forms of sales promotion. Their thinking, as mentioned before, is that window traffic represents a "circulation" similiar to that of advertising and could be regarded as apart from other sales promotion media.

Advantages of Using Window Display As A Separate Activity:

1. The selling productivity of each window can be more accurately evaluated.
2. Merchandise can be featured which is specifically suited to window display.

---

[12]For the purposes of this comparison we are considering *print advertising* only. We are not including radio, television or other advertising media.

Display

3. Windows can be kept more timely. For example, on rainy days the displays can feature umbrellas, rain boots, and raincoats.

Advantages of Using Windows in Conjunction With Advertisements:

1. The window could make it possible to reach customers who missed seeing the newspaper advertisement.
2. The repetition creates a strong impression on the customer that the store considers the merchandise and ideas featured as especially worthwhile.
3. Buyers have an incentive to develop bigger and more original promotions when they are promised the double-action impact of an ad *and* a window.
4. Many practitioners of sales promotion believe that consistent and repetitive emphasis on important merchandise will produce greater sales. They believe that advertisements and window displays used in combination are much more productive than either might be alone.

Some stores will try to duplicate the elements and the appearance of the ad in their window display (or vice versa).

Two Main Types of Window Display

The two main types of window display are *"selling displays* and *"prestige" displays.* "Selling" displays, like product advertisements, are designed to produce immediate sales by featuring the "right merchandise, at the right time, at the right price...." "Prestige" or institutional displays are designed to impress customers with the leadership and originality of the store rather than to stimulate an immediate purchase. The purpose of prestige windows is to convince customers of the desirability of this store as a place to shop. Prestige displays make their appeal through the newness, the fashion-rightness, the exciting assortments, and the timeliness of the merchandise.

Series and Related Displays

Series displays are those in which several adjoining windows are used to display a common merchandise theme. A series display for a store-wide French-import theme could feature: line-for-line copies of French designer dresses in one window, French leather gloves and handbags in the second, Parisian millinery in the third, boutique accessories in the fourth, and so on.

Related displays are those in which related merchandise is placed in one window; thus they tell a complete merchandise story. For the apparel departments, a related display might be designed around fashion information which indicates that beige will be a dominant color for fall costumes and ensembles. One window could thus feature costumes of beige dresses, beige coats, beige hats, shoes, and appropriate accessories.

Single category displays. Some retailers have found that related windows, while attention-compelling, often lack the selling impact of windows which concentrate on only *one category of merchandise.* In the latter, all attention is directed to a single type of merchandise at one price. The main objection to related displays is that they show so many different items that none get the emphasis and attention which concentration could provide.

Campaign Displays and Single-Promotion Displays

Campaign window displays are those in which the same type of merchandise is featured week after week in the same windows. The windows may change, but the merchandise category and keynote keep repeating a single sales message. For example, campaign displays can be effective in establishing a reputation for a particular item, brand or price line through repetition. The success of campaign displays demands that they appear in the same windows each week, and the design-style followed should have recognizable continuity.

Single-promotion displays are those in which one major selling event is featured in all or most of the store's windows. Most stores have traditional annual promotions which are important enough to assign all or most of its windows. Under the single-promotion display plan, all windows might be devoted to an annual "fall furniture festival," with displays of many different rooms of furniture and home furnishings.

Display

How Do Retailers Assign Windows?

There are two distinct policies which retailers use in assigning windows. One is the *departmental method* which assigns certain windows to certain departments for regular displays. The second is the *rotation method* which rotates windows from one department to another, attempting to expose the widest assortment of merchandise to customers. The method which is used depends upon the specific merchandising policy of the store. It is important that the windows reflect the store's attitudes toward merchandise and customer service. If a store's policy is to emphasize its concentration on certain price lines of apparel, then its major windows should feature these categories. Other merchandise would be assigned to windows which are not as prominently located.

If the store is trying to launch one of their own brands, this merchandise should be featured in the windows. When a store is known for doing an outstanding job in a certain department, this would encourage a policy which would constantly show that merchandise in the major windows. The assigning of windows is therefore a responsibility of those in the store who determine the store's fundamental merchandising objectives and service role to the consumer.

In specific situations the assigning of windows should also consider the following criteria:

1. The selling effectiveness of similar displays previously used.
2. Seasonal appeal and timeliness of merchandise.
3. Which categories of merchandise in which departments are being emphasized in the store's sales promotion plan.
4. The supplementary sales promotion activities which will be used.
5. The specific suitability for window display of this merchandise. . . .
6. Suitability of the merchandise for combination with merchandise from other departments in related displays.

7. The prestige which the store could receive from this particular display.

How Are Window Display Costs Determined?

Store windows are among the most valued areas of space in the store. The importance of window display as a salesman and traffic builder is universally accepted. Windows that face busy thoroughfares are especially prized. Their share of rent charged is usually higher per square foot than other areas in the store.

The general practice among retailers is to prorate the costs of display. These costs include: the specific rent charge for the window space, together with its proportional share of the costs of display props, fixtures and materials, the salaries of the display director and his staff, and the other variable costs such as lighting and maintenance. The "costs" of window display are charged to each selling department on a previously established proportionate basis. The criteria for "giving a buyer a window" is seldom based upon anticipated volume, since the windows are not as flexible a supply of sales promotion as advertising. For example, you can buy an extra page of advertising . . . .

How Often Should Windows Be Changed?

Surveys of retail stores in large cities have revealed that most stores change their window displays once a week. Stores in smaller cities will tend to changes windows more often. This is because the store in a small city at town, located in a compact business district, is likely to have its customers pass its windows more than once a week. On the other hand, the metropolitan store located in large, spread-out business area may not have people passing its windows even once a week. The exception would be those customers who are employed in the vicinity of the store.

Display

Regardless of location, however, each store must determine its own policy on frequency of change. The following questions related to the problems of the specific store could be asked:

1. What is the nature of the neighborhood location? — is it business or residential? A store in a residential section would have its windows seen more often by any one customer than a store in a business district.
2. What type of merchandise does the store carry — what is its "personality" and the nature of its service to customers? For example, is it necessary for a wallpaper and paint store to change its window displays as often as an apparel specialty shop?
3. How many people will pass the windows each day? A store located in a high traffic area might have to change its window displays more often.

What Are The Advantages of Frequent Change?

1. Displays can be more timely — tie-in with the most current fashion trends.
2. Customers are exposed to a greater variety of merchandise.
3. Merchandise is less likely to be damaged by soil and fading from the sun. Merchandise left in windows too long can result in expensive markdowns, if the merchandise gets soiled or faded.

Open and Closed Windows

A recent innovation in the design of new stores has been the use of "open" windows instead of "closed" windows. The open window eliminates the conventional closed-in compartment which we see in so many stores. The open or "see-through" windows permit customers passing by to get an unobstructed view of the interior of the store. The open window has been most popular with stores in shopping centers which depend largely on automobile traffic rather than passer-by traffic. The boosters of open windows maintain that customers of shopping centers (except those centers with networks of promenades) arrive with specific purchases in mind, leave their cars in near-by parking lots, and then go quickly to previously selected stores. There is no necessity or time for window shopping. Under these circumstances open-windows are all that are needed.

The open window has the following advantages:
1. It moves selling areas closer to the customer on the sidewalk.
2. An immediate impression of the interior of the store store is conveyed to the busy passers-by.
3. Customers can see the activity inside and may be impelled to "join in."
4. The initial construction and subsequent maintenance of open windows is less than closed windows.

There may be much to say for the open window in shopping centers that do not have public sidewalks. But many retailers still object to the "see through" window. They feel that the open window has the following disadvantages:

1. It is very difficult to emphasize a single item or an idea.
2. The open window does not permit as dramatic a merchandise or institutional display as the closed window.
3. It creates a "fishbowl" atmosphere in which customers and the interior of the store are "on view."
4. It reveals the interior of the store when it is empty, and may discourage customers from entering.
5. It gives up the stock space offered by the interior walls of closed windows.

The question of closed versus open windows necessitates the study of the advantages and disadvantages of each type. The type of store and its particular location are the main determinants. If a retailer expects a large volume of passer-by traffic, the closed window probably offers more possibilities for dramatic selling windows.

The Elements of Window Display

In the two-dimensional advertisement we are dealing with elements of art and copy which we arrange or "layout" into the space available. In window display we are using physical rather than graphic elements, arranging them in space for maximum attention and selling effect. These physical elements are: 1) The *Merchandise* itself, apparel and/or accessories. 2) *Functional props* which include mannikins and forms which "wear" apparel or abstract props or fixtures which hold merchandise. 3) *Decorative props* are used to establish a mood or setting for merchandise. 4) *Structural props* which support functional and decorative props, fixtures, mannikins or other units. Structural props are architectural in design and can change the organization and physical contours of the window. 5) *Backgrounds*. The back and side walls of the window (Discussed in detail later in this section). 6) A great variety of *Display materials* ... as wide a selection as creative imagination (and budget) will allow. These are used for floors, walls, decoration, pictorial setting and atmosphere.

In practice, the effective use of these elements is based upon the same criteria which apply in other sales promotion activities. The customer must be attracted, his interest aroused by merchandise (or ideas about it), and he must be given specific reasons to buy suggested by *his* wants and needs. The display director must use his creative skills to make display dramatic and attractive. His first responsibility, however, is to fulfill the buyer's and the store's sales objectives.

How is Balance Used in Window Display?

As in advertising layout, balance is an essential quality of a well-designed display. It involves the arranging of merchandise and props around the center in such a way that their weights will balance when they are equally distributed. Symmetrical balance is obtained by placing two objects of the same weight at equal distances from the center. Informal balance is obtained by placing heavier units toward the center and lighter ones away from the center. Formal balance arranges a large unit in the window's center of interest with the lighter units in harmony with it to provide symmetry.

Formal balance is used when it is desirable to have a dominant point of interest in the display with subordinate elements each having equal attention-power.

Informal balance is used when the units to be displayed vary their attention-power but are arranged in a dynamic balance. The difference in attention-power may be caused by shape, color, or arrangement. Informal balance lends itself to dissimilar units.

To achieve attractive balance in window display, one should also consider *proportion*. By proportion we mean: (1) the shape or size of one display unit as related to another; (2) the shape or size of the unit as related to the window itself. Windows are most interesting to the eye when space relationships and proportions are varied.

When units of different heights are used in window display, the general practice is to arrange larger units towards the rear of the window with smaller units or those which have intricate detail toward the front.

Color

Colors suggest many different things to people. There are certain responses to color which are generally assumed to be universal. For example, red suggests heat and fire ... excitement. Yellow suggests gayety and the sun. Green is cool and relaxing. Blue is soothing, like the sea and sky. White is usually associated with purity and cleanliness. Black and gray are neutral and are, therefore, well suited for walls and backgrounds. Other colors seem to blend into these neutrals.

Lighting

Natural daylight is largely composed of cool blue light, while artificial light is largely warm and yellow. In practice, display directors use yellow light for merchandise which is worn at night. Merchandise for daytime use can be shown under daylight blue lighting. Warm lighting acts to neutralize cool colors and intensifies warm colors. Cool light neutralizes warm colors and intensifies cool colors.

Backgrounds

The purpose of the background in window display is to provide the merchandise with a framework that will create an appealing mood or realistic setting which will demonstrate the use of the merchandise.

The two basic types of background are: (1) the *decorative* background and (2) the *pictorial* background. The decorative classification includes all *fixed* backgrounds, such as wood panels and draperies. It also includes *movable* backgrounds, screens, and panels. Decorative backgrounds are designed to serve as an ornamental framework for the merchandise. The pictorial backgrounds provide the merchandise with a realistic environment similar to theatrical scenery. It suggests when, where, and how merchandise can be enjoyed. This is why many display directors prefer it to the less dynamic decorative background.

A Checklist for Effective Window Display. Some guidelines to follow suggested by the experience of many display directors:

1. *Planning.* Good window display is a product of careful planning and scheduling. The components of an effective window need to be planned in advance with enough time for preparation and installation.
2. *The merchandise should be in demand.* Windows, just as much as advertisements, should feature merchandise in which customers have indicated high interest. What will be fast-selling is usually effective in windows. Merchandise with high impulse to buy will make the windows more productive, and customers will be impressed that the store has the right merchandise at the right time.
3. *Timeliness.* Window displays should be in tune with whatever is current. The display director should be alert to all that is happening in his area, in order to capitalize on events of public interest. For example, the opening of the opera season could suggest a theme for evening wear and accessories.

4. *The policy and character of the store should determine how much merchandise.* The right amount of merchandise for a window display is very important. There are no concrete rules concerning the number of items that should be featured. This depends upon the character of the store and what it wants to say to its customers. The important thing is that the merchandise should demonstrate, in assortment and quality, the basic appeal of the store itself.
5. *Merchandise should be suitable for window display.* A window display should not include merchandise which is out of proportion to its setting. Large pieces of furniture, for example, should be placed in a window large enough to enable customers to visualize how it might look in a room. Smaller items, such as fashion accessories, should be displayed in smaller settings, to prevent merchandise from looking lost in a disproportionate large space. Generally, bigger items should be placed further back from the glass and small items should be brought close to the glass so that important details can be examined by customers at comfortable eye-range.
6. *Simplicity.* Simplicity is a good general rule for all categories of design. Window display is no exception. An overworked, over-cluttered display works against its sales objective because it is not readily understood. The customer does not receive a single, emphatic impression.
7. *Lighting.* Lighting can be a key to effective or ineffective window display. Customers must be able to see merchandise clearly in order for it to arouse their interest and desire to buy. Inaccurately directed lighting creates glare and makes it difficult to see any of the units clearly. Improper distribution of light obscures certain units of display and creates unattractive shadows and too much reflection. If the display man wishes to emphasize certain units and de-emphasize others, he can direct his lighting accordingly.

Display

8. *Cleanliness and Order.* It goes without saying that the window must be neat and clean. It is surprising how many stores fail in this respect. Cleanliness in display involves more than the merchandise. Mannikins, props, fixtures, walls, flooring, glass and signs must be clean and in good order. Customers are repelled by cracked noses, crooked wigs and dead insects. Windows should be checked regularly (each day) to spot any imperfections in cleanliness and order.

When Should Signs and Prices Be Used?

Descriptive signs. Most stores believe that descriptive signs are an essential element to all window displays. Many stores have a policy that no merchandise can be displayed without descriptive signs. Signs can mean as much to a window as copy to an advertisement. A sign can present a merchandise theme, introduce a fashion trend, give the background of a product, tell why it is desirable, why it is an excellent value, and so on. Window signs can be printed or hand-lettered. They must follow the "look" of the entire display, much the same as typography style in an ad. The sign should be legible and easy to read. The copy should be concise and not attempt to go beyond one important keynote. Too many appeals can confuse the onlooker so that no message gets through. Generally, the principles for advertising copy would also apply in the writing of window signs.

Prices. Except for the certain exclusive shops, most stores follow a policy of pricing merchandise in their windows. Many stores control the emphasis that they place on price, by varying the lettering, shape, size and color of price cards.

Fashion Sales Promotion

THIS ILLUSTRATION REPRESENTS; A) SINGLE CATEGORY WINDOW DISPLAY; B) INFORMAL BALANCE; C) PICTORIAL BACKGROUND; D) BANNER-TYPE SIGN

IDENTIFY THE 6 DIFFERENT TYPES OF INTERIOR DISPLAY REPRESENTED IN THIS ILLUSTRATION.

Display

THIS ILLUSTRATION REPRESENTS:
A) CAMPAIGN WINDOW DISPLAY;
B) FORMAL BALANCE;
   FIXED DECORATIVE BACKGROUND;
D) EASEL AND HANGING-TYPE SIGN

THIS ILLUSTRATION REPRESENTS: A) A RELATED WINDOW DISPLAY; B) FORMAL BALANCE; C) FIXED DECORATIVE BACKGROUND; D) EASEL-TYPE SIGN

101

Interior Display

More and more stores now consider interior display to be one of their most important sales promotion activities. They regard interior display as a necessary partner of window display and advertising. Effective interior display can supplement those sales promotion activities which contact customers before they come to the point-of-sale. Interior display can act as a kind of insurance for the effort and expense of advertising and window display activities.

Why Do Stores Plan Interior Display?

1. *Location.* Interior displays help customers to locate merchandise which they have seen in windows and ads.
2. Interior displays *help salespeople to sell* merchandise by providing additional information and selling points to customers.
3. Interior display can *suggest a related item* to a customer and help salespeople to build a larger sale.
4. Interior displays give each department an opportunity to *bring its merchandise out where customers can see it*, sometimes providing the only sales promotion activity other than personal selling.
5. Interior displays can provide the store with a new *personality* for seasonal and store-wide events. This can be done throughout the store or in separate departments.

What Are The Different Types of Interior Display?

Most retailers find that their interior display problems are as individual as the character and physical facilities of their store. Each will develop his own methods and techniques.

Most interior display, however, can be classified as follows:

1. Showcase displays.
2. Counter displays.
3. Environment displays.
4. Wall, ledge, aisle and island displays.

Display

The department head can work with the display director to determine which kind of interior display will be most effective for his merchandise and department. He must analyze the department's space and traffic patterns and decide what are the sales objectives of his interior display. Interior display should be developed from the character of the merchandise itself as well as the look which the department head wants for the department.

1. *Showcase displays.* There are several kinds of showcase displays, all characterized by their *degree of accessibility to the customer*: (a) sides of selling cases where merchandise can be seen through the glass; (b) the glassed-in wall cases behind the counter where stock is kept but where merchandise is also visible; (c) shadow boxes: open, recessed areas above and behind the selling counter; (d) interior windows: usually built into spaces alongside doorways, elevator banks, escalators and staircases.

2. *Counter displays.* A display on a selling counter must be limited because of the danger that it might interfere with personal selling and obscure other merchandise which customers should see. There are other items beneath glass counters in cases which counter display should not hide. Counter displays are important and can be effective in helping salespeople to illustrate and convince customers of selling points necessary to create the desire to buy.

3. *Environment displays.* This type of display is basically different from the typical selling display. Of course, the purpose of both is to sell, but the approach is different. In the environment display, merchandise is placed in a *realistic, life-size setting,* which helps customers to imagine the satisfactions which they could obtain from owning it. Furniture, appliances, rooms, and even houses are featured in environment displays.

4. *Miscellaneous displays.* There are several other miscellaneous interior display techniques which stores use as their space and facilities allow:

Wall and ledge spaces can be utilized as display areas. Substantial amounts of unused wall and ledge spaces can be developed into effective and attractive store and departmental displays.

Island displays, like wall displays, can use to advantage areas of floor space which might otherwise be idle. Every store can find certain areas where traffic is light enough to permit free standing display units. When these are placed at the end of an aisle which comes to a dead-end, they are called *aisle* displays.

How does Interior Display Sell?

Any of the forms of interior display could be further classified by sales objectives:
(1) To present assortments; (2) To introduce ideas; (3) To suggest related merchandise.

1. *Presenting assortments.* An assortment display shows the customer a wide range of merchandise, which can include styles, colors, materials, and prices.

2. *Introducing ideas.* Displays which present background information, new uses and care of merchandise, the "romance" of the particular item or its designer, and so on.

3. *Suggesting related merchandise.* Related merchandise is grouped to promote an associate sale and help the customer visualize how certain items of merchandise will look and act with others.

Who Uses Signs and Prices?

The character of the store will largely determine whether interior signs and price cards should be used. Our previous discussion on signs for window display generally applies to interior display. Except for a few exclusive specialty stores, most stores use interior signs and prices.

The variety of signs used by stores include the following: (a) counter signs; (b) hanging signs; (c) banners and flags; (d) elevator cards; (e) posters; (f) easels.

Display

Who is Responsible for Window and Interior Displays?

The display responsibility in a retail store is divided between the merchandising and display divisions. Department heads are responsible for the selection of merchandise and themes which will satisfy the objectives of the store's Sales Promotion Plan. They must develop ideas which will sell merchandise *and* the store to the customer.

The display director and his staff are responsible for the translation of sales objectives into effective and attractive display design. The display must sell merchandise and the store. It must contribute to the prestige and personality of the store.

The display division is responsible for all window equipment, materials, signing, and maintenance. The staff designs, and executes window displays. They effect the unity and coordination of window display and store-wide interior display. This includes walls, columns, ledges, doorways, elevators and other "free areas" which are designed for store-wide display.

In many stores, department heads handle their own interior display, calling upon the display department for fixtures and signs. In this case a request is filed for whatever equipment and material is required, with the copy for the signs written by the buyer and his assistants. Departmental interior display, since it is concerned mainly with the arrangement and selling of merchandise, is often executed by experienced salespeople in the department, who have been assigned this responsibility by the buyer.

Often buyers will request *special departmental displays* which the display department can plan and execute. This is similar to the procedure used for requesting an advertisement or a window display. In cases where merchandise is loaned to the display division for other than departmental display, *loan slips* are used as a receipt for such merchandise. Thus merchandise which is outstanding for more than a prescribed period of time can be recorded and recalled.

Conclusion

Many retailers consider window and interior display to be of equal importance. The display departments of some large stores maintain separate interior display staffs and will assign a staff member to each floor or to certain departments. No matter what its size, no store can afford to be without display. The exceptions are some of the new "windowless" buildings which are constructed for stores who emphasize other sales promotion activities and attempt to presell their merchandise with extra-heavy advertising and publicity budgets. Such stores do less in interior display and their "selling from pipe racks" is incorporated as part of their image to customers. The general trend, however, is in the direction of more and better display. Many producers are using street-level showrooms and remote display to sell their products and ideas to buyers. They use their selling showrooms to feature interior display at the point-of-sale. The excitement of fashion apparel involves all of the senses — with sight and touch high on the list. Effective display allows one to see and feel and react to this excitement.

IV – PUBLICITY

Publicity is defined as: an *"unsponsored"* and *non-paid* message — verbal or written — in a public information medium, about a company, its products, policies, personnel, activities or services. It is a sales promotion activity.

Any discussion of publicity invariably includes two other terms which are incorrectly used as synonyms for publicity, and vice versa. These terms are *public relations and advertising*. The reader should understand that public relations, publicity, and advertising are related, but the differences between them are very fundamental. The following analysis indicates these differences and relationships.

Publicity can result either from events that are deliberately *created*, or from an alert *coverage* of an event which will occur that is of interest to a firm's various "publics". The *practice* of publicity does not rely on accidental happenings ... it *plans happenings*.

Unlike advertising, publicity cannot be controlled. Where, when, and how the message appears cannot be directed by the publicity director. His only "control" is in suggesting and informing publication editors of the happening of news which would be of interest to the publication's readers. The publicity practitioner who uses a professional approach, and submits news which is of genuine value to a publication's readers, has the best chance to get his message in the *editorial matter* of a publication.

Created or planned publicity is used or not used, subject to the judgment of the editor or columnist who receives the material. Where and how it is used — in a column — in a feature story — or as a separate news story — is the decision of publication editors.

For example, the same publicity material could be sent to several newspapers and magazines. It might well be treated in a very different way in each one. It could be developed as a feature story in a magazine, as a small news article in the fashion section of another, and be omitted from others. The distinction in any publication between *editorial matter* and *advertising* (or in radio or television, *entertainment* and *commercials*) is a most important one. Editorial matter consists of general news, features pages, special sections, and columns which are written and supervised by news editors, fashion editors, business editors and the like. Advertising is a paid message from any business or individual who cares to purchase the space. As long as an advertiser can pay for his ad, and comply with the *acceptability standards* of the publication, he can have his advertisement published. If a business or an individual knows of or develops an interesting "news angle" or news story about his firm, its products, policies or personnel — he can send it to editors for their consideration. Editors may include the story in the publication if they feel it is of genuine interest to their readers. An editor's job depends on sustained readership which results in circulation.

Public relations is not sales promotion. It is rather a long-range policy and program to create favorable public opinion about a firm. It is a sustained effort which serves as a guide for all communications with a firm's customers, vendors, employees or stockholders. As such, it helps set certain criteria for publicity, advertising, community relations, and the like.

A public relations *program* is concerned with everything that a firm does which will influence public thinking and attitudes. Publicity, advertising, and other sales promotion activities can be an important part of a public relations program

Publicity is a communications element of public relations.

Advertising can also be a contributor to a public relations program. In many firms where advertising is employed as the major contact with the customer public, it is most of the public relations program. Advertising involves the sending of sales messages through various media. The space for these messages is *purchased* from various publications such as newspapers and magazines; time is purchased from radio and television stations; postage is purchased for direct mail. Advertising is generally designed to produce sales. It is characterized mainly by the fact that it is paid for (sponsored), and therefore directly controlled by the advertiser.

The advertiser selects the medium and decides when his message will appear. He writes the copy and determines the art and layout. What the advertisement says, and how it looks, is his responsibility and under his direction.

Why is Publicity so Important?

One of the most popular misconceptions in sales promotion practice is that publicity is "free advertising". This is a serious error since the ultimate use of publicity material is not under the control of the interested party. Advertising and publicity are basically different in that advertising is a message *from* the interested party, and publicity is a message from an information medium *about* an interested party. Publicity and public relations can work to create a receptivity for a firm's advertising.

Publicity is a unique form of sales promotion because it involves the planning of a program to get influential columnists, commentators, publications and personalities to say interesting and complimentary things about the firm, its personnel, and its activities. It is one thing for customers to read and hear from the firm itself just how good it is. It is also very impressive to customers to hear such things from objective and authoritative sources.

Responsibility for Fashion Publicity

The responsibility for fashion publicity is usually left to the professional practitioner. More and more producers of textiles and apparel are beginning to recognize the value of a publicity program in their sales promotion effort. They are instituting new publicity departments or working with outside agencies and consultants. The large retailer is involved in a publicity effort which is handled by a special division or department. In many cases, (which we will discuss in a later section), the publicity program is combined with *special events* — especially on the retail level.

Although publicity programming and execution are the responsibility of the publicity department or agency, no firm could expect to do an effective job without additional help. This must come from those who know fashion and its customers most intimately. Buyers, salesmen, and fashion coordinators can contribute to the information and exposure which the publicist needs. For example, buyers help obtain photos from apparel manufacturers for their store publicity department. Buyers will also arrange editorial credits for their store, in magazines which are featuring fashions which they have bought for their customers.

Fashion coordinators are very publicity-conscious. They will work with the publicity department to develop publicity for their own clinics and fashion shows — and also to stimulate publicity for fashion trends which they consider important for their customers. In some firms, the responsibility for fashion coordination and publicity is incorporated in one department.

How do you get Publicity?

An understanding of what is news and how editors evaluate news for their own publications is most important for the publicity person. The trite and obvious "you gotta know the right people" is indeed a misconception on how publicity is obtained. Knowing *who* are the right people to send publicity material to, and maintaining continuous and friendly contact with them, *is* important. It is essential to have a knowledge of the layout and content of newspapers and magazines which reach your audience. An analysis of the average newspaper reveals that everything in it is not "news". The newspaper tries to give all of its readers good reasons to read its various sections and departments. Thus, each publication presents a varied menu of news, columns, editorial comment, special features, departments, feature pages, and supplement sections. The publicity practitioner's responsibility is to write for some part of the newspaper's editorial matter. The better acquainted he is with the requirements of the newspaper, or any other medium, the better he can develop his material for the medium's specific use.

What is the Nature of News?

A large part of the publicist's job is to develop a happening or event so that it becomes genuine news or is at least possessed of intriguing or entertaining aspects that will make for interesting reading. A "news angle" may have to be invented through imaginative thinking. For instance, bridal "promotions" come usually twice a year, but gowns seldom show great change. What could be done to "make a story" each time?

What type of fashion story is of genuine interest and value to readers of fashion pages and features? The following are general subjects which could serve as a guide for hundreds of different stories and features:

A new trend (boots instead of shoes)
An improvement (permanent-press fabrics)
A synthesizing of related matters (accessories appropriate for the weekends in the country)
A response to new ways of living (fashions for traveling, sailing, skiing, for private beaches or pools, skin diving, fishing or snorkling)
A major business move (opening a new suburban store, a newly redecorated floor, or a new department)
A "first" or an "exclusive" (a new designer for the Junior Deb Department)

Knowing what is the nature of news, and being able to recognize and develop a news angle into news story, is the first step towards obtaining publicity. The publicist must be an effective reporter, trained to dig for news. Understanding the needs of various publications will result in stories which can qualify as:

a) *Straight news* ... important, exciting happenings and events.
b) *Human interest* — stories of personalities, subjects which are meaningful to the life and welfare of the reader.
c) *Feature* — the unusual angle, the surprise twist — not necessarily long, but heavy on appeal to the reader.

The Publicity Outlets

The publicist must know *where* to send his story. A thorough knowledge of publicity outlets is valuable in a program to obtain publicity.

Newspapers — Leading daily and Sunday editions; Sunday supplements (Parade, This Week, American Weekly, New York Times Magazine); leading weeklies; trade newspapers (Women's Wear Daily, Daily News Record). The types of story for newspapers are (a) *general* — prepared for main news sections — announcements, new policy, special events, changes in administration or procedure; (b) *departmental* — slanted for a *specific section or column* — fashion pages, society, travel, food, entertainment, sports, business.

Magazines — General national *consumer* weeklies — Life; *News* weeklies — Time, Newsweek; *Women's Service* — McCall's, Good Housekeeping; *Home and Living* — Better Homes and Gardens; *Fashion* — Vogue, Glamour, Seventeen; *Trade* — Menswear, Sportswear Merchandiser. The special-interest story which is slanted to the selective audience of the magazine is more acceptable to magazine editors.

Radio — The rules for radio publicity are generally similar to newspaper publicity. The local interest or "home town story" is especially effective. Here, the style can be more informal, and the particular delivery of the commentator who will receive your material should be kept in mind.

Television — The most specialized and professional handling is required for television publicity. The skills of a specialist with considerable "TV knowhow" is usually needed.

In the placing of publicity material, the publicist must plan and write with the *type of story* or coverage firmly in mind. The *content* of his story — personal interview, fashion product news, fashion trends, institutional information ... will help determine the type of story. The publicity material prepared will be designed for a newspaper column, special section, editorial, general section — or a magazine feature, department, photo layout — for a radio or TV personality or commentary show.

The Contacts — It is always important to have contact with "the right people". This does not mean that responsible editors can be influenced by bribes or cajolery to grant special publicity favors. An editor who abdicates his responsibility by putting personal interests ahead of those of his reader, listener or viewer does not last very long on a reputable medium. It is important for the publicist to know who the editors and reporters are, when or where they can be reached, and the type of material they want and need. It is also important that editors and reporters know the publicist personally, and a friendly but professional relationship should be developed. A telephone should be used to give the press "tips" when appropriate. Whatever a publicist can do to help keep a publication informed will be returned in kind when a "break" on a story is requested. It is always good practice to include photographs with captions to accompany press releases, articles and features. It is frequently "guesstimated" that three-fourths of all editorial matter is suggested or "planted" by the interested party. The publicist's material, sent on a *consistent basis* to the *right person* at the *right time*, will be used when it is good, and when there is *room for it*. The professional publicity person does not need to plead with or pressure editors and reporters. He should be helpful, patient, courteous and productive. He should keep good material coming, as much and as often as possible.

The Press Release

The press release is the most-used vehicle for transmitting publicity material from publicists to editors. Its format, style and contents vary, but certain elements are common to all. The press release illustrated here, is a good example of the most generally accepted format, and the reasons should be obvious to the reader:
   A. All copy is typewritten on 8½ x 11 white paper; no onion skin.
   B. The format for the first page follows the style below:
      Name of Company or Agency   For Release
      Address: Street, City, State   (DATE)
      Telephone
      Name of writer
         HEADLINE IN CAPS, UNDERLINED
     Lead sentence starts about half way down the page.
   C. Double space copy, with at least a one inch margin left and right.

Name of Company or Agency   For Release
Address: Street, City, State   (DATE)
Telephone
Name of writer

HEADLINE IN CAPS, UNDERLINED

Lead sentence starts about half way down the page.

###

Style of the Press Release

D. Write on one side only; all pages numbered after first page; the word "more" is put at the end of each page until story ends.
E. Paragraphs should not be broken; end paragraph on same page. *Repeat key words of headline* at upper right of each page after first.
F. At end of story, put end mark — ### or —30—.
G. *One story* on a page only. Wherever possible, stories should be sent SPECIAL or EXCLUSIVE.

> *SPECIAL* — written specially for a publication.
> *EXCLUSIVE* — no other paper gets this story.
>
> Fashion photographs *must* be exclusive for each editor even if background story is not.

H. First class mail should be used rather than mass mailings.

Content and Style of the Press Release—*The headline:* The headline should present a capsule of the prime news interest of the story. It is not an attempt to write a headline for the publication. This is an editor's job. It should be concise and emphatic. It should include an action verb. *The subheadline:* this is optional and is used when it is necessary to supply an additional important fact. *The lead:* usually a sentence or two which summarizes the news including the *who, when, what, where and why*. Should an editor need to "edit" or cut a story even to the lead, the essence would still remain.

The next sentence or paragraph begins to fill in the story. Throughout the release, facts should be used in *order of diminishing importance.*

Editors want facts, not opinion, and can detect instantly a "build-up" for something really insignificant. The truth should be told. Honesty in publicity material will generate good will with editors. Clean-cut statements with full data, such as complete names and titles (sometimes with addresses too, in parentheses afterward) make for professional releases. It is better to include too many, rather than too few facts, as long as they are arranged in a quick-to-grasp and easy-to-edit format. An editor can cross out words, but should not have to spend precious time calling the writer for fill-in data. This applies especially in New York and other large cities, where newspapers almost invariably rewrite the story according to their own approach, so as to avoid duplication of what others are running. Copy in a release should be as near in style to the publication as possible. The publicist must determine what the publications want and give it to them.

Clarity of set-up for the release is most necessary to an editor whose desk each day is piled high with all kinds of communications. He must scan through these at top speed, and a format which enables him to grasp the story fast is a sign of professionalism, and is appreciated.

Photographs — Fashion photographs are usually prepared with the format and visual style of particular publication in mind. Most of the fashion publications and special sections have staff photographers who have developed individual styles and techniques for their own editors. When photographs are included with press releases or other publicity material, the following general requirements should be observed:

A. Size, 8" x 10", or 5" x 7", glossy stock
B. Avoid "busy" backgrounds — emphasize people and fashions.
C. Captions should be typewritten and attached securely.
D. Identify back of photograph in case attached identification is lost.
E. People should be identified from left to right. Full names, titles, firm affiliations are always included.
F. Written releases should be obtained from all models and people in photographs.
G. Credit all syndicated or stock news service photos; others as required.

The Timing of Press Releases

Some stories are *advance announcements*. In this case verbs are in the future tense.

e.g. "Macy's will open Resort World on Monday, April 27 . . ." The publicist must beware of making assumptions which may prove false, such as, "a large, enthusiastic audience". A snow storm could keep an audience home, and one can only *hope* for an audience's enthusiasm.

Some stories can only be *reviews*. "Sales for the 52 week period ended January 31, 1971, were $50,000,000, the highest in the store's history."

Publicity

```
FROM:  SARONG, INC.                    FOR IMMEDIATE RELEASE
       200 Madison Avenue
       New York City  10016
       New York

CONTACT:  Marjorie Vaughan
          PL 9-1900, Ext. 30

              SARONG INTRODUCES HAWAIIAN COLLECTION

    Aloha excitement themes this dreamy duet, ideal underscoring
    for festive fashion.  Sarong fashions the petticoat in an
    exclusive Hawaii print on polyester chiffon in Blue, Rose
    or Gold.  A filmy hem of misty lace is scalloped in Sand
    color.  Short, Demi or Average lengths in Sizes Petite,
    Small, Medium and Large, about $10.00.  Sarong designs
    the matching push-up bra for functional fit, fashion appeal.
    A natural, with deep-see necklines.  Sizes 32-36 in A-B-C
    cups, about $10.00.  Available at (store name) in November.

                             # # #
```

Illustrated is a typical fashion photograph with caption attached.

Careful thought should precede a specific release dating. Any necessity for a *particular date of publication* makes news perishable. Who would plan a big Saturday fashion story for a Thursday when papers usually devote the woman's page to foods? If the story fails to make the Thursday page, it is dead. Saturday events are too late for Sunday, and dead for Monday. These should be written in future tense and released in advance for a *Friday* publication.

Some stories can be released for "Immediate" use, as an *exhibit of period furniture* which will last for several weeks, an *interview with a store personality*, or simple brief "fillers" about newsworthy but small individual items.

There is nothing as old as "yesterdays news". It is the responsibility of the publicity writer to consider the timeliness of his news and to give a release dating which will allow the editor to present the story as close to the happening as possible.

The Language of Publicity — Publicity writing should not be treated in a subjective manner. It should be written in the *third person; you, I* or *we* is never used! The writing should be handled as if the publicity writer were not an interested party, but rather an objective reporter. It is not *advertising copy*, which has a completely different purpose. It is not a literary composition, an essay, or a philosophical dissertation. These will rarely make the daily paper!

Editors want facts and reject such words as "marvelous", "fabulous" and superlatives which are opinion and overrate the facts. They also do not react favorably to last year's trite or hackneyed expressions.

This does not mean that the writing has to be sterile. Fashion is more than a utilitarian covering. Fashion is more than seams and darts and textiles. Fashion is a "look", a mood, a coordination, a living art. A vivid evocation of mood may, in its proper place, be considered factual reporting about fashion. This can be achieved through verbs and allusions, through solid writing rather than through an avalanche of adjectives. The active verb conveys far more spirit than passive forms. Some nouns hold a world of overtones. A look through any of the popular consumer fashion magazines will illustrate how richly expressive the language is. There are fashions in words used to describe color, style, silhouette.... The arts, history of costume, languages and theories of color all lend depth of perception and a new range of illusion to the writing of fashion.

Editorial Credits

When publicity materializes for the manufacturer, it is the obligation of the editor to inform his readers of retail locations where the merchandise may be purchased. The naming of these stores in such publicity is an editorial credit. Editorial credits may also include the names of designers, manufacturers, and often the suppliers of various accessories. It is of extreme importance that when an editorial credit appears, the merchandise should be available in the stores listed.

Conclusion

Publicity, like every other activity in sales promotion, must be planned on a consistent basis. It must be properly executed by professionals who know how to "create" as well as "cover" the news. It should not be an activity which relies on the accidental incidence of news. The alert firm which considers publicity as a *program* — and is willing to evaluate its achievements over the long run — will institute this activity as an important factor in its sales promotion effort. A continuing effort, conditioned by realistic appraisal of *customer interest*, will usually give results which justify the continued effort.

V. FASHION SHOWS

Of all the activities in the sales promotion of fashion, the fashion show stands out as the most dramatic and compelling. When it comes to presenting the excitement and glamour of fashion, no other form of selling can compete with a fashion show. The reason for this is implied in the name and definition of a fashion show itself. It is a show. In every sense of the word. Every element of theater is incorporated together with its devices and its procedures. The fashion show can be simply defined as: "A promotional medium that presents merchandise in living and moving form."

The fashion show, like all other sales promotion activities can take many different forms. It also "plays to different audiences." It has different sponsors and different uses.

Why is the Fashion Show important to the Fashion Industry?

One of the most popular current theories in effective selling is the one which counsels—"If you want to sell—influence the influentials." There is something about the fashion show with its advance notices, first opening, and theatrical production, which makes its audience feel influential. The effective show can generate in its audience a feeling of being let-in-on the newest and most important developments in the world of fashion. The very successful shows have an "in-crowd" audience fighting for admission, creating a syndrome of excitement which carries through the coming season. This occurs on all market levels: the "haute couture" in Paris with its profes- and apparel producers; the consumer shows of prominent retailers. Despite the limitations in audience size (as compared to other activities using public information media) the fashion show's power to influence those who influence others — the designers, the buyers, the retailers, the press and the in-customers — make it a most important sales promotion activity.

Among the important reasons for staging a fashion show are prestige, the introduction of new lines and designs, and the building of good will. Frequently a fashion show is given to impress a public of the store's fashion alertness and leadership.

Types of Fashion Shows

There is very little agreement on terminology in this area. Many sponsors of shows will call their productions fashion shows which others would consider as merely "showings" or informal shows. For the purpose of clarity we will classify fashion shows as "Formal" or "Informal".

The Formal Show is a show with an identifiable theme; a staged production, a script and commentary. It generally has an invited audience which is usually seated. It incorporates all or most of the elements of theater.

The Informal Show or "Showing" is a presentation whose theme is not as emphatically identified as in the formal show. It relies on a comparatively loose structure with production, staging and direction not as tightly planned and rehearsed as in the formal show. The informal show does not always have a script and commentator — the audience reads descriptive information from cards or programs.

The difference in the two types of shows is mainly a matter of degree. They both rely on some theme, some sort of descriptive commentary, some production and staging. When the production is "all-out theatre" we consider it a formal show. When a more informal structure is used, we consider it an informal show or showing. In most cases, *strict* classification could be a problem.

The Audience and the Sponsor

Both formal and informal fashion shows are used by each of the market levels in the fashion industry. Each is playing to its own audience; each has its own sales objectives. Fashion shows can also be classified by sponsor and audience.

Fashion Sales Promotion

The Trade Show is sponsored by a producer of raw materials (usually textiles) or a producer of apparel. The audience is usually composed of professionals and/or the press. In the case of the raw materials producer, the audience will include apparel designers, piece goods buyers for apparel producers, retailers and the press. The objectives of such shows are to demonstrate the versatility, utilization and appropriateness of the material product in the designing and manufacture of fashion. The apparel designer and producer will play to an audience of retailers and the press with the objective of selling their interpretation of fashion trends and tastes. He seeks to differentiate his product and his line in terms of originality and value appeal to the consumer. Several of the prominent consumer fashion magazines also sponsor shows which, in effect, could be called trade shows. Sometimes referred to as *fashion clinics*, these shows present fashions from many apparel producers which represent the magazine's editorial viewpoint on what is important and exciting, and which they hope will be featured by their editors. The audience will frequently include many levels of the fashion industry: raw materials and apparel producers and retailers, and members of the non-competitive press.

The Retail Show is sponsored by the retailer for presentation to many different types of audience. Each of these has a different objective which might have very little effect on its structure. The *internal* or *in-store show* is designed to inform store personnel of the what's new and exciting which the store will promote. Its purpose is to acquaint its audience with the merchandise, stimulate their enthusiasm, suggest selling points and sales approaches. It serves to implement sales promotion planning throughout all levels of the store. The *customer show* is a presentation to customers which features store-wide, seasonal, departmental, designer, private label, or manufacturer-brand themes. It is designed to sell merchandise, and ideas which sell merchandise. Manufacturers will cooperate or provide the elements for a consumer show which features their line exclusively, or presents their line with some prominence. They will send special sales representatives to present "trunk showings" of merchandise to customers in the store, in advance of the selling season. These are very informal and are usually presented right on the selling floor.

The *community* or *charity show* is co-sponsored by the store with a local institution or fund-raising charity. The objectives, in addition to selling the merchandise, are institutional — increasing good will, and building a strong community position.

The Press Show is a special performance for members of the press usually given in advance of the "regular performance." This is a practice of the larger trade and retail sponsors who wish to ensure themselves of substantial press publicity.

Fashion Show Budgets

Probably the most important factor in a successful fashion show is the process of thoroughness in planning. No detail may be left to chance and no phase of the show should be presented without rehearsal.

In planning a fashion show, the end consideration of course, includes audience, size of audience, and purpose of the show. An experienced producer of fashion shows would quickly admit that the show depends heavily upon the budget. Depending upon many factors, every fashion show does not have all of the following items to be considered in a budget, but it is well to use some type of check list to be certain that there is budget to cover the following:

1. Rent (if any)
2. Porters
3. Transportation
4. Stage and Runway Construction
5. Curtains
6. Electricians
7. Props
8. Advertising and Publicity
9. Lights
10. Public Address System
11. Alterations
12. Pressing
13. Tickets
14. Posters
15. Programs
16. Model Fees
17. Commentator Fee
18. Overtime
19. Meals
20. Music
21. Depreciation of Merchandise
22. Insurance

Fashion Sales Promotion

How Do You Do A Good Show?

The following is an adaptation from "Let's Have A Fashion Show," used here by special permission of Sears-Roebuck & Co.

It is an excellent guide to the planning, procedure and division of responsibility for the production of a fashion show. The example used here is from the retail level — but the guidelines apply to any level.

I. You Need a Theme — It isn't enough just to collect a lot of clothes and parade them in front of an audience without rhyme or reason. They need to be held together by some common *theme*. This is your excuse for showing them at all. This is what you hang your advertising and your publicity on. According to its timeliness, interest and the effectiveness with which you *tell your story* (or detail your *theme*) your show will be successful or it'll be a dismal failure. Themes are derived from many sources. Some of the obvious ones are: seasonal themes, Easter fashions, occasion themes, vacation time, particular type themes, the career girl, travel themes.

II. You Need a COORDINATOR — The Coordinator is your key person. She must be endowed with fashion know-how, patience, tireless enthusiasm ... and a *fashion show staff*. She must have a capacity for detail, and a willingness to take over practically any part of the job herself ... from outfitting "Miss America" to sweeping out the fitting room. If a firm does not have a staff fashion coordinator, then an outside specialist should be retained to work with management.

The Coordinator's major responsibilities are:

A. *Appointing her staff*, which should include someone from each of the apparel areas, to handle major garments — dresses, coats and suits, sports and leisure wear — someone who will be responsible for all accessories; an alteration hand, several assistants to serve as dressing room workers, and someone who will be responsible for the pressing of the garments. In addition, the Advertising Publicity and Display departments should be kept informed of the theme selected, colors to be featured and all pertinent information.

B. *Developing the theme* in terms of actual merchandise.

C. *Discussing with the Department Head* the merchandise which will be needed; he will have knowledge of what merchandise is on order, and when it will be in. If this does not cover the show's requirements, the department head should arrange for additional merchandise, in a range of colors and sizes, and should authorize withholding from stock merchandise already ordered.

D. *Arranging time and place* for fitting the models. There is always a room available somewhere in the store — not less than 20 feet square where your racks, garments, alteration woman, models and coordinator can be centered. She'll do the fitting in far less time, and do a better job.

E. *Working closely with the accessories representative* during the fittings. As the coordinator sees the garment on the model she can write out her accessorizing suggestions, and the representative of the accessories departments can carry them out. It is important in accessorizing group showings that accessories be carefully selected to present a diversified accessory story.

F. *Keeping descriptive notes* for the commentary, to be written and delivered by herself, or by whoever has been selected as commentator.

G. *Making merchandise and model sequence charts* for rehearsal and show.

H. *Setting up rehearsal arrangements*, and acquainting each committee member with his or her responsibilities. All models and assistants should be told the exact time and place of the rehearsal, and of the show and the approximate length of time their services will be required.

I. *Assigning a responsible person* to getting the models on and off stage on time, working as liaison between the commentator on stage and the dressing room backstage.

J. *Arranging for music* for rehearsal and show.

III. You Need an AUDIENCE It is necessary to select just the right audience from the point of view of potential good customers for your Fashions. You must also ensure that there will be a large enough attendance to make all the time and effort and expense worthwhile.

IV. You Need a PLAN Don't attempt a fashion show without a well-organized plan of what you're going to do every step of the way. This plan will include date, place, length of the show, its theme, how many models, who the audience will be, what merchandise will be shown, and so on.

Length of show — This is important since it will determine the number of models you'll need to show a pre-retermined number of garments.

Generally speaking, 45 minutes should be the maximum length for a show.

In this time you can show 50 to 60 garments depending on the number of models and their degree of proficiency.

Audience — If you are presenting the show under your own auspices, take all necessary steps to make sure your have a guaranteed audience. If a sponsoring group is involved they must guarantee a minimum audience.

V. You Need MERCHANDISE All merchandise shown should fit into the theme of the show; e.g., Easter fashions would not include swimsuits. But Easter fashions would, very properly, include coats, suits, small fur pieces, dresses, skirts and blouses, and these would all be carefully accessorized with items from the proper departments. If children are included, the appropriate garments would be selected from their divisions.

VI. You Need MODELS And here are some possibilities: professional models; former models; your own employees — you might have some who've had some instruction; your sponsoring group; design school students; college students; members of "Little Theater" group; dance school students. How many models? This is determined by the number of garments you plan to show. *Eight* is generally the minimum if you have professional models. Their sizes should be 9, 10, 11 and 12. If you're staging your style show for a group, such as

Fashion Shows

Mother's Guild or PTA or Junior League, it is usually best to use members as models, as this guarantees greater interest, cooperation and attendance. Here you may wish to use twelve models in assorted sizes. A good size breakdown in a lineup of twelve models is: four juniors, sizes 9 and 11; six misses, sizes 10 and 12; one mature woman with an ample, well-proportioned figure; and one model in a half size.

Models' height should be at least 5'5" in their stocking feet if garments are to be shown to advantage and with the least necessity for costly and time-consuming alterations. In working with volunteers from the sponsoring group try tactfully to select those with the best figures. But, if the first vice-president is eager to model, accept her anyway.

VII. You Need a BUDGET It costs money to give a fashion show. Once you've been given the authority to *plan* (not *give*) a show, it is wise to set down on paper your estimate on what the show should cost. Get an OK on this figure from whomever will pay the bills. Use these items as a guide to total cost.

VIII. You Need STAGING Some of the elements of successful staging are: a stage or ramp or runway; theatrical lighting; music; public address system; background displays (or scenery); props.

Your *display man* is a logical person to be responsible for these items. If the show is in a store he must plan the *stage* (or runway) so that the *dressing rooms* are easily accessible and so that the models can get to the stage and back to the dressing room with minimum confusion.

IX. You Need DRESSING SPACE It should be *sufficient* to accomodate the models who are wearing your fashions, and the "assistants" you have assigned to help them dress and change. It should have one or two *full-length mirrors*, plus other adequately lit mirrors where makeup may be applied and hair fixed. It should have *racks* for the garments you are going to show, as well as *racks* or *hooks* for the models' own clothing.

X. You Need a COMMENTARY The coordinator may also be the commentator. And sometimes it is good to turn the commentary over to a local celebrity, such as the newspaper's Woman's Page editor, or the emcee of a Women's radio or TV program. In this case the commentary is often supplied to her by the coordinator. Don't let the term "Commentary" scare you. And if *you* are delegated to be the commentator, take confidence from this:

Every time you make a sale, you're telling your customer what a garment will do for her — where she can wear it — what its particular advantages are, from a style or care viewpoint. Your audience is that customer, multiplied by perhaps 200 — or even 500. But the important thing for you to remember is that you're telling the story to a customer — not "making a speech" or striving to sound like fashion copy.

Be prepared to "*ad-lib*" some fashion gems, to fill in any pauses that might occur between models' appearances. Perhaps something about skirt lengths, or a color trend, etc.

XI. You Need a PROGRAM As soon as the model sequence has been made definite, you are ready to write up your program. This can be as simple as an 8½ x 11 sheet of paper, folded once, giving you four 8½ x 5½ "pages." Mimeographed listings, with prices, are really sufficient.

Your sponsoring group may want to plan a more elaborate program, listing their committees and officers. You then give them the fashion listing information as early as you have it ready.

XII. You Need a REHEARSAL A run-through including all the people concerned with the show is absolutely necessary. In a show to be held in the store, it is obviously impractical to rip the departments apart to provide the space that will be used on the show night. However, the training room can be arranged to approximate the conditions. At this time, the listing sheet should be in everyone's possession. If there are any inconsistencies, or if a model finds she cannot make a change fast enough to meet the schedule (although this should all have been worked out previously) all these things now have a chance to be solved.

XIII. You Need PROMOTION . . . *and GOOD PUBLICITY* . . . Promotion includes: posters, invitations, and tickets. Publicity: advance announcement; stories of the show, the fashions, the designs, the personalities in the audience.

If you're putting on a fashion show, don't keep it a secret. Go after an *audience* aggressively.

FASHION OFFICES:

Fashion offices are often operated by manufacturers, stores, and resident buying offices. A fashion coordinator or director is responsible for the communication of fashion information. She predicts fashion and color trends to come, based upon research and experience.

The fashion coordinator must also study consumer markets and consumer wants and needs; develop sources of fashion information; prepare written market reports and forecasts; establish fashion promotional programs; coordinate color, silhouette, fabric into exciting fashion stories; spot new items, resources, design ideas; coordinate merchandise groups and accessories; plan and conduct fashion shows; plan promotional material.

The fashion office is important to all levels of the fashion industry. It is the research and development department of a fashion firm.

Conclusion

The fashion show is unique because it is alive and mobile. The audience is seeing fashion being worn by very attractive people who are evidently enjoying the appearance and feel of it. There is considerable difference in the way you see a chiffon dress on a window mannikin, and the way you see it flow through space as a model moves across a stage.

For those who work with, wear, and appreciate fashion — the fashion show can create magic. And this fashion show magic sells ... It presents creative talent in textile and apparel design; introduces new expression; launches trends; suggests how to merchandise; influences customers to buy; stimulates publicity.

VI. SPECIAL EVENTS and FEATURES

Special Events are specific devices, features, services, sales inducements, exhibits, demonstrations and attractions which are used to influence the sale of merchandise or ideas. In order to meet the growing competition in the fashion industry, firms have developed new methods of selling prospective purchasers. They have supplemented their advertising, publicity and display with other forms of sales promotion which we shall call special events.

Frequently two or more of the events may be used in combination. Sometimes, for example, a *merchandise* special event and an *institutional* special event may be combined by presenting an expert or consultant to give demonstrations of merchandise. Celebrities may be invited to appear as commentators or as models at fashion shows; or to serve on panels or as judges in customer or employee contests. Almost invariably firms seek to obtain press publicity for their special displays and exhibits or other such merchandise and institutional special events. This is a very important objective of the special event. Many firms in the fashion business link their publicity and special events programs because of this close relationship. The following are five categories of special events used by producers and retailers in the fashion industry:

A. *Merchandise Events*
  1. Product displays and exhibits
  2. Demonstrations and showings
  3. Schools and classes

B. *Institutional Events*
  1. Parades
  2. Shows (Fashion, Flower)
  3. Sponsorship of athletic teams (Bowling, Little League Baseball)
  4. Celebrity visits
  5. Lectures

    6. Consultants — (Bridal, College)

C. *Free Samples of Merchandise*
D. *Special sales inducements*:
    1. Premiums — (Special Offers)
    2. Special Conditions of Sale — (August Fur Lay-a-Way Sale)
    3. Contests (Customer and Employee)
    4. Give-a-Ways — (Good-will specialties, The Shopping Bag, Re-use Packaging)
E. *Customer Advisory Boards.* (Consumer Panels, College Boards, Career Boards).

The growing importance of special events. The numerous devices used on each of the market levels differ widely in nature; but they all are used to accomplish one of more of several general sales objectives. When used by retail stores, they are expected to attract customer "traffic" — to draw large numbers of customers to the store where they will be exposed to the merchandise and ideas the store wants to sell. Stores in metropolitan locations use these events to attract customers to "come on downtown." The events also serve to impress customers that the store is a community headquarters for a variety of educational and entertaining events. The special event endeavors to develop in customers, the habit of visiting the store regularly and often.

Manufacturers can use special events to accomplish the same objectives of increasing *showroom traffic and interest* in products and services they offer. They also use the event as an integral part of a program to obtain advantageous product and institutional publicity. Retailers have generally done more to develop new and diversified special events because of their constant effort to keep customer traffic high and continuous.

Conclusion

Some retailers have separated their effort into a separate *Special Events Division*. The responsibility for special events promotion as mentioned previously is sometimes combined with that of publicity. The size and diversity of a firm's special events program would determine whether it needs a separate department to handle it. As in the other sales promotion activities, advertising and sales promotion agencies, consultants and free-lance specialists are equipped to plan and to execute such events.

VII. PERSONAL SELLING

Personal Selling is unqestionably the one selling activity that every merchandising or marketing group dwells on year after year. This activity seems to pose the one greatest problem at every level of the industry. Executives state the objective of improved selling but too often have no answer to the question of *how*. Any book which would pretend to offer a ready solution to the development of consistently good personal selling would itself have instant success. This section offers no sure remedies.

By experience, study, and evidence, one factor looms clear far too often. Poor supervision and poor management are generally behind poor selling. The education, training, supervision and constant programming of sales personnel development can be a key to the success of a business.

How often have you heard a customer (maybe yourself), leave a retail store with the remark, "I'll never set foot in that store again!" The point here is that the salesman or saleswomen represents the entire organization to the customer. The customer has no other contact. Therefore, this section on Personal Selling is not intended for the exclusive use of the training department, but rather for *any* aspiring executive of any company at any level of the industry.

A planned program for continual and informative sales training is essential to the success of a business. All the activities which precede this chapter are of little or no value if we fail in this one vital final activity. Whose job is sales personnel development? It is a combination of management, promotion, and merchandising division.

Management coordinates the program and provides basic training in procedures and policies. How to write up a sale — store policies with regard to services, returns, exchanges, guarantees, and such basic knowledge some under the responsibility of the management division. The promotion division plans and executes store-wide sales contests, campaigns, and programs for intensified efforts to stimulate better selling.

The merchandising division through merchandise managers, but principally through buyers and assistant buyers, has a two-fold responsibility. One is to inform the sales personnel about every item in the department. This means education in detail of what each product does or does not, its merits, its content, its benefits to the purchaser.

The second, a most important job to be performed by merchandise executives, is the stimulation of enthusiasm, that most elusive, most contagious, most effective element in selling. It should be remembered that lack of knowledge about a product is often the deterrent to enthusiasm.

Personal selling is defined as: An oral presentation in conversation with a prospective customer which is used to influence the sale of merchandise, services or ideas. The following will concern personal selling on the retail level. The techniques discussed generally are applicable to any market level.

There are two types of retail selling in current practice. These are: *simplified selling* and *personalized salesmanship*. Simplified selling is a general term that is currently used to describe the various methods of *putting customer in more direct contact* with merchandise. These methods reduce, or in some cases, eliminate the number of salespeople. Personalized salesmanship implies the situation in which a salesperson initiates the customer's contact with the merchandise and completes the sale.

Each of these two types has inherent advantages and disadvantages. The advantages of simplified selling are:

1. *It reduces the retailer's selling cost.* Many stores which feature low price merchandise and work on lower margin find simplified selling is a must.
2. *It is more efficient* for certain types of retail operations which feature certain categories of merchandise. For example, merchandise which is already packaged, and pre-sold through extensive sales promotion.
3. *It is actually preferred by many customers* — ("Self-service is a retailing way of life today".)

Personalized selling has these advantages:

1. *Some customer groups prefer* personal attention and service. They are interested in counsel and advice. They want someone to answer their questions, demonstrate features and suggest uses.
2. *Salespeople may suggest additional merchandise* and make "extra" sales more efficiently than self-service fixtures can. Salespeople can explain merchandise features that are not always too obvious by demonstrating the merchandise in use. Salespeople can complete sales that have been initiated by other sales promotion activities, such as display, advertising, publicity and fashion shows.

What is Salesmanship?

The purpose of salesmanship is to help customers to buy what they want and that which will give them satisfaction. The experienced salesperson will not be passive in his approach to his customers wants. He presents selling points and appeals which are designed to stimulate those wants. He is prepared to make suggestions to customers who are not sure what they want. He is also ready to "service" those customers who come to the point-of-sale with a fixed idea of what they want. The effective salesman does not persuade customers to buy what they do not really want.

Importance of "Salesmanship" for Fashion Merchandise

Many businesses are asking today; "Are salespeople necessary? — How much personal selling does my business need? — What "Sales promotion mix" do I use — heavy advertising, display, and self-serve with light personal selling — or vice versa?" There is no simple answer to this question. Any form of selling involves a *selling and buying process*. This process, (previously mentioned as the *AIDA procedure*), can be implemented entirely by personal selling — or in part by personal selling. The other sales promotion activities can bring the customer to the "last three feet" up to the point-of-sale. Advertising, display and publicity may have pre-sold this customer. In some cases, all the salesperson has to do is close the sale. It is the nature of a business, the character of its merchandise and the class of its customers which determine the "sales promotion mix".

Personal Selling

The selling and buying process.
A. Get "Attention" of customers.
B. Create "Interest and Desire" for product or service that is being offered.
C. Stimulate to 'Action" — get customer to buy it.
D. Customer "Satisfaction" — to avoid returns and assure repeated patronage.

WHAT SALESPEOPLE MUST KNOW —
A. Know their product and understand its important qualities of the merchandise from customers' viewpoint.
B. Know customers and what they expect from salespeople — e.g., service and/or information and/or advice.
C. Know what is in stock in order to find it quickly.
D. Understand today's customers — educated, affluent, impulse buyers who are too busy to waste time. They know what they want, have relatively little store "loyalties", switch "brands" easily. They are too sophisticated to be talked into merchandise that they do not want. The philosophy of "Caveat Emptor", (let the buyer beware), is being challenged by the current — "the consumer is king".
E. Understand the retailer's viewpoint — "The customer is always right."

SOME GENERAL "PRINCIPLES OF SALESMANSHIP"
A. The customer's viewpoint is the primary consideration in selling procedure. The salesperson is well advised to tell customers those things which they most want to hear about the merchandise.
B. Customers should be given reasons why they should buy. They want to be told "what will it do for me?"
C. The selling conversation should avoid the mechanical and obvious. The "canned pitch" is not acceptable to today's customers.

Procedures in personal selling:

1. Approach — the opening recognition and greeting to the customer (to get her Attention).
2. Determining customers needs and wants (to enable salesperson to develop customer's Interest).
3. Presentation of merchandise and development of selling points (to create Desire).
4. Meeting and overcoming customers' objections (if any).
5. Closing the sale and stimulating customer Action.
6. Suggesting additional merchandise.

Customers should not be "typed", in terms of price, probable intentions to buy, and the like.

The truth is still the best basis for any communication. It should be used in personal selling.

SPECIFIC SELLING TECHNIQUES

Approaches— meeting the customer: (getting her attention and interest) Of the main approaches, the *greeting* and the *merchandise approach*, the merchandise approach is generally more effective in getting customer's attention and arousing her interest. This involves an opening which mentions merchandise of interest to the customer.

Approaches which can too easily bring forth a negative response such as, "May I help you?" make it too easy to say "no". A simple greeting, such as, "good morning", is preferable to these.

Determining customer's needs and wants
  A. The salesperson should be alert to the customer's reactions to merchandise.
  B. He should listen to what customer has said and is saying.
  C. He should ask a very minimum of questions, (e.g., it is unwise to ask the price that the customer wants to spend).

Some Guidelines to the presentation of merchandise and development of selling points —

A process of *"Show and Tell"* to Create interest.

A. Merchandise should be presented as promptly as possible.
B. The customer is impressed when salespeople handle

merchandise with appreciation.
C. The customer is confused by being shown an "excessive" amount of merchandise.
D. The salesperson should start by showing medium-priced merchandise from which he can trade-up or down, depending on customer's reactions.
E. Merchandise should be shown in use whenever appropriate.
F. An appeal to the customer's senses should be attempted. Customer should be encouraged to touch merchandise.

Give selling points simultaneously with presentation to create desire.
A. A customer should be told what she most wants to hear about merchandise.
B. The salesperson should give *reasons to buy* by telling her "what it will do for her".
C. The salesperson should emphasize those qualities which are most desirable from the customer's point-of-view (e.g., suitability, utility, economy, variety of uses). Too many points, however, will confuse a customer.
D. The positive should be emphasized with a benefits "highlighted".

Meeting and overcoming objections

Some common objections by customers are: resistance to price, requests for out-of-stock items, "just-looking", "indecision" and so on.

Some recognized techniques for overcoming objections are:
A. Answer objections before they are raised by watching customer's reactions.
B. Do *not* argue with customer.
C. Admit objections and point out a superior feature.

Stimulating action to buy — "closing the sale"
1. Cease showing additional merchandise.
2. Narrow the selection and concentrate on those items in which customer shows great interest. (Remove others).

3. Use stimulators which can produce a decision:
   a. Present alternatives — e.g., "Which do you prefer?"
   b. Suggest decision — e.g., "Do you wish to charge this?"
   c. Assume decision — e.g., "You've made a wise choice"

The salesperson should avoid high-pressuring and hurrying the customer before she is ready.

Suggestion Selling

Suggestion is not substitution — it is a method of increasing a sale by: a) suggesting related merchandise, b) suggesting larger quantities of same merchandise, c) suggesting "specials" and/or advertised merchandise.

Suggestions can be made more emphatic by showing the merchandise rather than asking if the customer would "like to see something else".

Conclusion

The sales promotion problem of all firms on all market levels is fundamentally similar. Each business has the individual problems of defining its own objectives and policies; determining the class of customer it can serve best; deciding upon the character and extent of the merchandise and services it will offer; selecting the forms and media for sales promotion, which will do the best job of attracting and selling customers.

It is difficult sometimes to distinguish the specific characteristics which make one firm superior to another. Yet, no business can achieve any great success unless its performance is either different or better in some way than its competition. The purpose of sales promotion is to keep customers aware of the better job a firm is doing for them. A business must differentiate its value to its customers, and then with stimulating and informative sales promotion, keep this impression going strong.

NOTES

NOTES

NOTES

NOTES